The Merry-Go-Round by D.H. Lawrence

A PLAY IN FIVE ACTS

For many of us DH Lawrence was a schoolboy hero. Who can forget sniggering in class at the mention of Women In Love or Lady Chatterley's Lover? Lawrence was a talented if nomadic writer whose novels were passionately received, suppressed at times and generally at odds with Establishment values. This of course did not deter him. At his death in 1930 at the young age of 44 he was more often thought of as a pornographer but in the ensuing years he has come to be more rightly regarded as one of the most imaginative writers these shores have produced. As well as his novels he was also a masterful poet and wrote over 800 of them. Here we publish his plays. Once again Lawrence shows his hand as a brilliant writer. Delving into situations and peeling them back to reveal the inner heart.

Index Of Contents

Characters
MRS HEMSTOCK
NURSE BROADBANKS
MR HEMSTOCK
HARRY HEMSTOCK
BARON RUDOLF VON RUGE
THE BAKER, JOB ARTHUR BOWERS
MRS SUSY SMALLEY
DR FOULES
RACHEL WILCOX
BARONESS VON RUGE
MR WILCOX

Schedule
ACT I
SCENE I: Downstairs front room of the Hemstocks' cottage
SCENE II: Kitchen of the Hemstocks' house

ACT II
SCENE I: The same

ACT I

SCENE I

The downstairs front room of a moderate-sized cottage. There is a wide fireplace, with a heaped-up ashy fire. The parlour is used as a bedroom, and contains a heavy old-fashioned mahogany dressing-table, a washstand, and a bedstead whose canopy is missing, so that the handsome posts stand like ruined columns. The room is in an untidy, neglected condition, medicine bottles and sickroom paraphernalia littered about. In the bed, a woman between sixty and seventy, with a large-boned face, and a long plait of fine dark hair. Enter the parish NURSE, in uniform, but without cloak and bonnet. She is a well-built woman of some thirty years, smooth-haired, pale, soothing in manner.

MRS HEMSTOCK: Eh, Nurse, I'm glad to see thee. I han been motherless while thou's been away.

NURSE: Haven't they looked after you, Mrs Hemstock?

MRS HEMSTOCK: They hanna, Nurse. Here I lie, day in, day out, like a beetle on my back, an' not a soul comes nigh me, saving th' Mester, when 'e's forced. An' 'im. (She points to mirror of dressing-table.)

NURSE: Who is that, Mrs Hemstock?

MRS HEMSTOCK: Canna ter see 'im? That little fat chap as stands there laughing at me.

NURSE: There's no little fat chap, Mrs Hemstock.

MRS HEMSTOCK: There is an' a'. He's bobbing a' thee now.

NURSE, who has been rolling up her sleeves, showing a fine white arm, throws her rolled cuffs at the mirror.

NURSE: Then we'll send him away.

MRS HEMSTOCK: Nay, dunna thee hurt him. 'E's nowt but a little chap!

NURSE: I'll wash you, shall I?

MRS HEMSTOCK: Tha nedna but gi' me a catlick. I'm as snug as a bug in a rug.

NURSE (laughing): Very well.

She goes into the kitchen.

MRS HEMSTOCK (calling): Who's in there, Nurse?

NURSE: There's nobody, Mrs Hemstock.

MRS HEMSTOCK: I bet he's gallivanting off after some woman.

NURSE (calling): Who?

MRS HEMSTOCK: Why, our Mester. 'E's a ronk 'un, I can tell you. 'As our Harry done it?

NURSE: Done what, Mrs Hemstock?

MRS HEMSTOCK: Cut 'is throat. 'E's allers threatenin'!

NURSE (entering with a jug of hot water): What! You're not serious, Mrs Hemstock.

MRS HEMSTOCK: Aren't I? But I am. An' 'e'll do it one o' these days, if 'e's not a'ready. I 'avena clapped eyes on him for five days.

NURSE: How is that?

MRS HEMSTOCK: Eh, dunna ax me. 'E niver comes in if 'e can 'elp it.

NURSE: How strange! Why is it, do you think?

MRS HEMSTOCK: Summat's gen 'im mulligurles. 'E'll not live long.

NURSE: What! Harry? He's quite young, and has nothing the matter, has he?

MRS HEMSTOCK: You know, Nurse, I 'as a fish inside me. I wor like Jonah back'ards. I used ter feel it floppin' about in my inside like a good 'un, an' nobody'd get it out

NURSE: But Harry hasn't got a fish in his inside

MRS HEMSTOCK: 'E 'asna, but I believe 'e's got a leech.

NURSE: Oh!

MRS HEMSTOCK: Dunna thee wet my 'air, Nurse, it ma'es it go grey.

NURSE (smiling): Very well, I'll be careful. But what makes you say Harry has a leech in his inside?

MRS HEMSTOCK: On 'is 'eart. 'Asn't ter noticed 'e gets as white-faced as a flat fish? It's that.

NURSE: Oh, and did he swallow it?

MRS HEMSTOCK: 'E didna. 'E bred it like a mackerel's head breeds maggots.

NURSE: How dreadful!

MRS HEMSTOCK: When you've owt up with you, you allers breed summat.

NURSE: And what was up with Mr Hemstock?

MRS HEMSTOCK: With our Mester?

NURSE: With Harry.

MRS HEMSTOCK: You knowed, didna you, as 'e'd had ructions wi' Rachel Wilcox?

NURSE: No.

MRS HEMSTOCK: Oh, yes. 'E fell off 'is bike eighteen month sin', a'most into her lap, an' 'er's been sick for 'im ever sin'.

NURSE: But he didn't care for her?

MRS HEMSTOCK: I dunno. 'E went out wi' 'er for about twelve month, but 'e never wanted 'er. 'E's funny, an' allers 'as been.

NURSE: Rather churlish?

MRS HEMSTOCK: No, 'e wor allers one o' the' lovin' sor' when 'e wor but a lad, 'd follow me about, and "mammy" me.

NURSE: But he got into bad ways

MRS HEMSTOCK: Well, I got sick of him stormin' about like a cat lookin' for her kittens, so I hustled him out. 'E began drinkin' a bit, an' carryin' on. I thought 'e wor goin' to be like his father for women. But 'e wor allers a mother's lad, an' Rachel Wilcox cured him o' women.

NURSE: She's not a nice girl.

MRS HEMSTOCK: 'E'd only ter stick 'is 'ead out of the door an' 'er'd run like a pig as 'ears the bucket. 'Er wor like a cat foriver slidin', rubbin' 'erself against him.

NURSE: How dreadful!

MRS HEMSTOCK: But I encouraged 'er. I thought 'e wor such a soft 'un, at 'is age, a man of thirty!

NURSE: Was he always quiet?

MRS HEMSTOCK: Eh, bless you. 'E'd talk the leg off an iron pot, once on a day. But now, it's like pottering to get a penny out of a money box afore you can get a word from 'im edgeways.

NURSE: And he won't come to see you.

MRS HEMSTOCK: Not him! 'E once had a rabbit what got consumption, an' 'e wouldn't kill it, nor let me, neither would he go near it, so it died of starvation, an' 'e throwed a hammer at me for telling him so. You see, harsh! That's our Mester.

NURSE: Yes. Do I hurt you? They've let your hair get very cottered.

MRS HEMSTOCK: Get it out, Nurse, never mind me.

Enter MR HEMSTOCK, a very white-haired old man, clean-shaven, with brown eyes. There is a certain courtliness in his quiet bearing.

MR HEMSTOCK: I'm glad to see you back, Nurse, very glad. (He bows by instinct.)

NURSE: Thank you, Mr Hemstock. I'm pleased to see you again.

MRS HEMSTOCK (to her husband): Tha'rt not 'alf as glad to see her as I am. 'Ere I lie from hour to hour, an' niver a sound but cows rumblin' and cocks shoutin'. An' where dost reckon tha's been? Tha's been slivin' somewhere like a tomcat, ever sin' breakfast.

MR HEMSTOCK (to NURSE): I've been gone ten minutes. (To his wife.)I've on'y been for a penn'orth of barm ter ma'e thee some barm dumplings.

MRS HEMSTOCK: An' wheer's our Harry?

MR HEMSTOCK: He's in garden, diggin'.

MRS HEMSTOCK: What are ter out o' breath wi'?

MR HEMSTOCK: I've been runnin' our Susy's kids. They was drivin' our fowls again.

MRS HEMSTOCK: Tha shouldna ha' wanted ter come here, a mile away from anybody but our Susy.

NURSE: It is rather lonely, only Mrs Smalley's farm and your cottage. And the children are rather wild.

MRS HEMSTOCK: Let me live in a street. What does colliers want livin' in country cottages, wi' nowt but fowls an' things shoutin' at you or takin' no notice of you, as if you was not there?

MR HEMSTOCK (to NURSE): We came for the garden.

NURSE: I suppose you are still on strike.

MR HEMSTOCK: There's talk of settlement. I see they're opening some of the pits. But I've done, you know.

NURSE: Of course you have, Mr Hemstock. Harry will be glad to begin, though.

MR HEMSTOCK: I'm afraid whether 'e'll get a job. You see

MRS HEMSTOCK: What hast got for dinner?

MR HEMSTOCK: Roast pork, rushes, barm dumplings.

MRS HEMSTOCK: Then look slippy about gettin' it ready. I'm clammin'. Ha' thy heels crack.

MR HEMSTOCK (to NURSE): You wouldn't think she'd been bedfast thirteen month, would you?

MRS HEMSTOCK: Tha nedna ha'e none o' thy palaver wi' Nurse. Nurse, ta'e no notice o' a word 'e says. (HEMSTOCK goes out.)

MRS HEMSTOCK: He's a good cook, and that's all you can say for him.

NURSE: I think he's very good to you, Mrs Hemstock.

MRS HEMSTOCK: He's too busy runnin' after a parcel o' women to be good to me.

NURSE: If all men were as good

MRS HEMSTOCK: Tha's niver had him to put up wi'. Tha's niver been married, 'as ter?

NURSE: No, Mrs Hemstock.

MRS HEMSTOCK: A man's fair enough to you' face, if 'e's not as fow as a jackass; but let you' back be turned, an' you no more know what's in his breeches an' waistcoat than if 'e wor another man.

NURSE: Oh, Mrs Hemstock!

MRS HEMSTOCK: Yes, an' tha'll "oh" when tha knows.

NURSE: I'm sure you're getting tired. Won't you have your bed made?

MRS HEMSTOCK: Sin' it's gone that long, it might easy go a bit longer.

NURSE: Why, when was it made last?

MRS HEMSTOCK: How long has thee been gone away?

NURSE: Three weeks.

MRS HEMSTOCK: Then it's that long.

NURSE: Oh, what a shame! Wouldn't Mrs Smalley do it?

MRS HEMSTOCK: Our Susy! 'Er'd better not show 'er face inside that door.

NURSE: What a pity she's so quarrelsome! But you will have it made?

MRS HEMSTOCK: I know tha'll whittle me to death if I dunna. Does tha like roast pork?

NURSE: Fairly. Now, shall I lift you onto the couch?

MRS HEMSTOCK: No, tha wunna. I want na droppin' an' smashin' like a pot. I'm nowt but noggins o' bone, like iron bars in a paper bag. Eh, if I wor but the staunch fourteen stone I used to be.

NURSE: You've been a big woman.

MRS HEMSTOCK: I could ha' shadowed thee an' left plenty to spare. How heavy are ter, Nurse?

NURSE: I don't know, about ten and a half stone. Will Mr Hemstock lift you, then?

MRS HEMSTOCK: I say, Nurse, just look under the bed, atween th' bed slats at th' bottom corner, an' see if tha can see th' will.

NURSE (doubtful): What! (She stoops dubiously.)

MRS HEMSTOCK: Right hand corner. I told the doctor to put it there. Canna ter see it?

NURSE: Oh, yes, here it is. (She reappears with an envelope.)

MRS HEMSTOCK: That's it, it's fastened safe. It's a new will, Nurse. I made 'em do it while tha wor away, doctor and Mr Leahy.

NURSE: Oh, yes

MRS HEMSTOCK: An' I'm not goin' ter ha'e none on 'em gleggin' at it. I know our Susy often has a bit of a rummage, but I'm sharper than 'er thinks for.

NURSE: And what shall I do with it, Mrs Hemstock?

MRS HEMSTOCK: Why, get upon th' table, an' look if there isna a hole in top o' the bedpost, at th' head there, where a peg used ter fit in.

NURSE (climbing up): Yes, there is.

MRS HEMSTOCK: Then roll it up, an' shove it in. On'y leave a scroddy bit out.

NURSE: That's done it, then.

MRS HEMSTOCK: Tha'll know where it is, then. Tha ought, tha's been more to me than any of my own for these twelve month.

NURSE: Oh, Mrs Hemstock, I hope

MRS HEMSTOCK: Nay, tha nedna, tha'rt knowin' nowt, I tell thee. How much dost reckon I've got, Nurse?

NURSE: I don't know, Mrs Hemstock.

MRS HEMSTOCK: Over five hundred, I can tell thee. I made 'em in a little shop as I had in Northrop when the colleries hadna started long, an' I did well, an' so did our Mester, an' so 'as th' lads done

NURSE: It is a good thing, for now they're both out of work they'd have nothing.

MRS HEMSTOCK: Oh, our Harry's got a bit of his own, an' our Mester's got about a hundred. It'll keep 'em goin' for a bit, wi'out mine.

NURSE: You are queer, Mrs Hemstock.

MRS HEMSTOCK: Ha, that's what they say about th' Almighty, they canna ma'e Him out. But I'll warrant He knows His own business, as I do.

NURSE: Oh, Mrs Hemstock.

MRS HEMSTOCK: Yes, an' I want my bed makin', dunna I? Shout our Harry. Harry! Harry!

After a moment, HARRY enters: a man of moderate stature, rather strongly built: dark hair, heavy, dark moustache, pale, rather hollow cheeks, dangerous-looking brown eyes. A certain furious shrinking from contact makes him seem young, in spite of a hangdog, heavy slouch.

HARRY (to his mother, in broad dialect): What's want?

MRS HEMSTOCK: I s'd think it is "What's want" an' I hanna set eyes on thee for pretty nigh a week. Tha'll happen come to lie thyself, my lad, an' then tha can think o' me hours an' hours by mysen.

HARRY: What's want?

MRS HEMSTOCK: An' why art paddlin' about in thy stockin' feet for? Tha 'asna gumption enough ter put thy slippers on, if ter's been i' th' garden. Nurse, gi' me a drop o' brandy. (She lies back exhausted. NURSE administers.)

NURSE: Your mother wants lifting onto the couch, Mr Hemstock. (He comes forward.) Perhaps you will wash your hands in this water, will you (He obeys sullenly.)

MRS HEMSTOCK: Tha'd better wesh 'em for 'im, Nurse, 'e's nowt but a baby. 'As 'er catched thee yet? (He does not answer.) 'E dursna go round th' corner, Nurse, for fear of a bogey, durst ter, eh? 'E's scared to death of a wench, so 'e goes about wi' a goose.

A goose comes paddling into the room and wanders up to HARRY.

NURSE: Hullo, Patty! You dear old silly.

MRS HEMSTOCK: Dost like 'er, Nurse?

NURSE: She's a dear old thing.

MRS HEMSTOCK: Then tha'll like him. He's just the same: soft, canna say a word, thinks a mighty lot of himself, an's scared to death o' nowt.

NURSE: Oh, Mrs Hemstock!

MRS HEMSTOCK: I canna abide a sawney.

NURSE: Are you ready, Mr Hemstock?

He comes forward. NURSE wraps Mrs Hemstock in a quilt.

MRS HEMSTOCK: To think as I should be crippled like this!

NURSE: Yes, it is dreadful.

HARRY lifts his mother, NURSE showing him how.

MRS HEMSTOCK: Tha's got fingers like gre't tree-roots.

NURSE shows him how to place his hands. Then she lifts the trailing quilt and follows him to the couch.

MRS HEMSTOCK (rather faintly): I canna abide to feel a man's arms shiverin' agen me. It ma'es me feel like a tallywag post hummin'.

NURSE: There, be still, you are upset. I'm sure Mr Hemstock did it gently.

She stoops and strokes Tatty, who is crouched near the bed. HARRY moves as if to go.

Will you fetch clean sheets and pillow slips, be quick, will you?

HARRY goes out. NURSE begins to make the bed.

MRS HEMSTOCK: Isna 'e like that there goose, now?

NURSE: Well, I'm sure Patty's a very lovable creature.

MRS HEMSTOCK: I'm glad tha thinks so. It's not many as can find in their heart to love a gaby like that.

NURSE: Poor Patty!

MRS HEMSTOCK: An' that other hussy on'y wants him cause she canna get him.

NURSE: It's often the case.

MRS HEMSTOCK: It is wi' a woman who's that cunning at kissin' an' cuddlin' that a man 'ud run after 'er a hundred miles for the same again.

NURSE: Is she clever, then?

MRS HEMSTOCK: She melts herself into a man like butter in a hot tater. She ma'es him feel like a pearl button swimmin' away in hot vinegar. That's what I made out from 'im.

NURSE: She's not a nice girl.

MRS HEMSTOCK: An' 'e hated her cause I shoved him at her.

NURSE: But you don't care for her, surely.

MRS HEMSTOCK: Canna bear her. A pussy cat always rubbin' 'erself agen a man's legs, an' one o' the quiet sort. But for all that, I should like to see him married afore I die. I dunna like, Nurse, leavin' 'im like 'e is. 'E wor my darlin'.

NURSE (softly): Yes.

MRS HEMSTOCK: An' 'e niver wor a drunkard, but 'e's the makin's of one.

NURSE: Surely not, oh, how dreadful!

Enter HARRY with bedding. He helps NURSE shake up and make the bed.

NURSE: How sweet the sheets are! They were aired on the currant bushes. Did Mrs Smalley wash them?

MRS HEMSTOCK: Our Susy! Not likely. She'd never do a hand's turn. I expect our Harry there weshed 'em, an' 'is father. Dunna look so; canna ter answer a bit of a question? (He does not answer.) 'E looks as if 'e'd swallowed a year o' foul weather.

NURSE: Hem at the top. (She stumbles over Patty.) Oh, poor Patty, poor old bird! Come here then, you dear old thing, did I hurt you?

MRS HEMSTOCK: Tha's more fondness for that goose than I han, Nurse. It's too much like him. Birds of a feather flock together.

NURSE: You include me.

MRS HEMSTOCK: If tha likes.

NURSE: It's not a compliment.

MRS HEMSTOCK: It isna. Tha'rt a lady, an' han a lady's time, an' tha'rt a fool if tha changes.

NURSE: I am not so sure

MRS HEMSTOCK: Tha gets a good wage, an' th' minute tha enters a house everybody gets up to run about after thee. What more dost want?

NURSE: I don't know.

MRS HEMSTOCK: No, I s'd think tha doesna.

NURSE: Sometimes I get tired, and then, I wish, I wish I'd somebody to fad after me a bit. I nurse so many people, and

MRS HEMSTOCK: Tha'd like nursin' thysen. Eh, bless you, a man's knee's a chair as is soon worn out.

NURSE: It's not that, I should like a home of my own, where I could be private. There's a lonely corner in most of us that not all the friends in the world can fill up

MRS HEMSTOCK: And a husband only changes a lonely corner into a lonely house.

NURSE: Perhaps so. But I should like to be able to shut my own doors, and shut all the world out, and be at home, quiet, comfortable.

MRS HEMSTOCK: You'd find you shut the door to stop folks hearing you crying.

NURSE (bending down and stroking Patty): Perhaps so.

MRS HEMSTOCK: Tha art fond o' that bird.

NURSE (flushing): I am.

MRS HEMSTOCK: If I wor thee, our Harry, I wouldna let Patty beat me, even.

HARRY: What dost mean?

MRS HEMSTOCK: Stroke him, Nurse, and say "Poor old Harry".

NURSE: Mr Hemstock will have a grudge against me if you slate him so in my presence.

MRS HEMSTOCK: And would it grieve thee?

NURSE: I should be sorry.

MRS HEMSTOCK (after a pause, vehemently): Ha, if he worn't such a slow fool! Can thee lift me back, Nurse?

NURSE: Won't you let Mr Hemstock?

MRS HEMSTOCK: No, thee do it.

Exit HARRY.

Did ter niver ha'e a sweetheart, Nurse?

NURSE: Yes, when I was in the hospital. He was a doctor.

MRS HEMSTOCK: An' where is he?

NURSE: He was too good for me, his mother said, and so

MRS HEMSTOCK: Tha'rt well rid o' such a draggletail. How long is it since?

NURSE: Eight years.

MRS HEMSTOCK: Oh, so tha'rt none heartbroken. We'n got a new assistant. I like him better than the owd doctor. His name's Foules.

NURSE: What!

CURTAIN

Time: the same. The kitchen of HEMSTOCK'S house, a large, low, old-fashioned room. Fowls are pecking on the floor. HARRY, in a coarse apron, is washing the floor. MR HEMSTOCK, at the table, is mixing flour in a bowl.

MR HEMSTOCK: Who wor that scraightin' a bit sin'?

HARRY: Our Susy's kid.

MR HEMSTOCK: What for?

HARRY: I fetched him a wipe across th' mouth.

MR HEMSTOCK: There's more bother then

HARRY: He was settin' that dog on th' fowls again.

MR HEMSTOCK: We s'll be having her round in a tear, directly, then.

HARRY: Well, I'm not

There is a knock: and in the open doorway at the back a little, withered, old clergyman, the BARON, is seen.

BARON: How is the sick woman this morning? (He speaks with a very foreign German accent.)

MR HEMSTOCK: I think she's middlin', thank you.

BARON: I will go and see her, and speak to her.

HARRY: We've told you a dozen times 'er na wants you.

BARON: It is my duty that I shall go

HARRY (rising from his knees): Tha are na!

BARON: I am the vicar of this parish. I am the Baron von Ruge. I will do my duty

HARRY (confronting him): Tha'rt na goin' to bother her. Her na wants thee.

BARON: Stand clear of my way, sir, I will go, I will not be barred, I will go to her, I will remind her

HARRY (frustrating his efforts): 'Er na wants thee

He suddenly moves: the BARON rushes into Patty. The goose flaps and squawks and attacks him. The BARON retreats hastily. Enter NURSE.

NURSE: Whatever is the matter?

MR HEMSTOCK: It's Patty haulin' the Baron out

NURSE: Oh dear, how dreadful!

MR HEMSTOCK: 'E's bin plenty of times, an' every time our Harry tells 'im as Missis won't be bothered wi' him

NURSE: What a pity she won't see him. Don't you think if you let him go

HARRY: Ask 'er thysen if 'er wants 'im, an' if 'er doesna want 'im, 'e's na goin'

NURSE: But what a pity!

MR HEMSTOCK: You can't make heads or tails of what 'e says. I can't think what they want wi' a bit of a German Baron bein' a vicar in England, in this country an' a', where there wants a bluff man.

NURSE: He's a Polish nobleman, Mr Hemstock, exiled after fighting for his country. He's a brave man, and a good gentleman. I like him very much.

MR HEMSTOCK: He treats you as if you was dirt, an' talks like a chokin' cock

HARRY: An' 'e's na goin' pesterin' 'er when 'er doesna want 'im.

NURSE: Well, of course you know best, but don't you think Mrs Hemstock ought to see a minister? I think

Enter the BAKER, a big, stout, pale man of about forty.

BAKER: Been havin' a shindy with the Baron?

MR HEMSTOCK: He wants to see the Missis, an' we not let him.

BAKER: You'd best keep th' right side of 'im. (He swings his large basket, which he carries sackwise on his shoulder, down to a chair.) The strike is settled, an' th' men's goin' back on the old terms.

NURSE: Oh, I'm so glad.

BAKER: Fisher's a deep 'un. The Company'll know yet as they've got a manager.

NURSE (to HARRY): So you'll be going back to work soon, Mr Hemstock. You will be glad.

MR HEMSTOCK: Me, I s'll never work again. An' it's doubtful as our Harry won't get on

BAKER: They gave you a place before the strike, didn't they, where you had to work you inside out for about fifteen shillings a week?

HARRY: Ha.

He goes out.

MR HEMSTOCK: Yes, they treated him very shabbily.

BAKER: I bet it was th' owd Baron. He's a good hand at having your eye for a word, an' your tooth for a look. I bet Harry'll get no job

MR HEMSTOCK: No, I'm afraid 'e wunna. The Baron will go down to Fisher

BAKER: And Harry can go down to, his godfather, eh, Nurse?

NURSE: I don't understand.

BAKER: Old Harry.

MR HEMSTOCK: I hope to goodness 'e will get something to do, else 'e'll mope himself into the cut, or the 'sylum, afore long.

BAKER: Oh, it's love what's upset him, isn't it? Rachel Wilcox was too much for his stomach

MR HEMSTOCK: I dunno what it is.

BAKER: She's a bit of a ronk 'un. She was his first cigar, an' it's left him sick yet. She's not half bad, you know, if you can stand 'em strong.

NURSE goes out.

I've scared Nurse off. But Harry's got a bit of a thin stomach, hasn't he? Rachel's not a half bad little ha-p'orth.

MR HEMSTOCK: Some's got a stomach for tan-tafflins, an' some 'ud rather ha'e bread an' butter

BAKER: And Rachel's creamy, she's a cream horn of plenty, eh, what?

MR HEMSTOCK: A bit sickly.

BAKER: I dunno, it 'ud take a lot o' rich food to turn me. How many?

MR HEMSTOCK: One of yesterday's bakin', please.

BAKER sets the loaf on the table.

BAKER: Your Susy wa'nt in, I wonder what she wants. Where is she, do you know?

MR HEMSTOCK: She'll be somewhere lookin' after th' land.

BAKER: I reckon she makes a rare farmer.

MR HEMSTOCK: Yes.

BAKER: Bill left the place in a bit of a mess

MR HEMSTOCK: A man as drinks himself to death

BAKER: Ay! She wishes she'd had me astead of him, she says. I tell her it's never too late to mend. He's made the hole, I'll be the patch. But it's not much of a place, Smalley's farm?

MR HEMSTOCK: It takes her all her time to manage an' pay off Bill's debts.

BAKER: Debts, why, I thought from what she said

Enter SUSY SMALLEY, a buxom, ruddy, bold woman of thirty-five, wearing thick boots and a dark blue milkmaid bonnet.

MRS SMALLEY: Wheer's our Harry?

MR HEMSTOCK: I dunno. 'E went out a bit sin'

MRS SMALLEY: An' wheer is 'e? I'll let him know whether he's

Enter HARRY.

Oh, I've foun' thee, have I? What dost reckon tha's been doin' to my lad?

HARRY: Tha nedna ha' hunted for me. I wor nobbut i' th' garden.

BAKER: You should ha' looked in th' parsley bed, Susy.

MRS SMALLEY: That's wheer to find babies, an' I'll baby him. What did thee hit my lad for?

HARRY: Ask thysen.

MRS SMALLEY: I'm axin' thee. Tha thinks because I hanna a man to stand up for me, tha can

HARRY: There's a lot o' helpless widder about thee!

MRS SMALLEY: No, an' it's a good thing I'm not helpless, else I should be trod underfoot like straw, by a parcel of

HARRY: It's tha as does th' treadin'. Tha's trod your Bill a long way underfoot, six foot or more.

BAKER: It's a fat sight deeper than that afore you get to blazes.

MRS SMALLEY: Whatever our Bill was or wan't, 'e was not a' idle skilk livin' on two old folks, devourin' 'em.

NURSE (entering): Oh, think of your mother, Mrs Smalley.

MRS SMALLEY: I s'll think of who I like

BAKER: An' who do you like, Susy?

MRS SMALLEY: You keep your "Susy" to yourself

BAKER: Only too glad, when I get her

MRS SMALLEY: An' we don't thank Nurse Broadbanks for interferin'. She only comes carneyin' round for what she gets. Our Harry an' her's matched; a pair of mealy-mouthed creeps, deep as they make 'em. An' my father's not much better. What all of 'em's after's my mother's money.

NURSE: Oh, for shame, for shame!

HARRY: Shut thy mouth, or I'll shut it for thee.

MRS SMALLEY: Oh, shall you? I should like to see you. It's as much as you durst do to hit a child, you great coward, you kid.

MR HEMSTOCK: Shut it up, now, shut it up!

MRS SMALLEY: But I'll let him know, if he touches my child again; I'll give him what for. I'll thrash him myself

BAKER: That's your brother, not your husband.

MRS SMALLEY: I will an' a'. Him an' his blessed fowls! 'E's nobbut a chuck himself, as dursn't say boh to a goose, an' as hides in th' water-butt if his girl comes to see him

HARRY dashes forward as if to strike her. The BAKER interposes.

BAKER: Here, none o' that, none o' that!

MRS SMALLEY: A great coward! He thinks he'll show Nurse Broadbanks what he is, does he? I hope she'll storm round him after this bit.

HARRY (in a fury): If tha doesn't

MR HEMSTOCK: Let's have no more of it, let's have no more of it

BAKER: How much bread, Mrs Smalley? I reckon your Bill bettered himself when he flitted, what? I don't think. How many loaves? I saved you a crusty one.

MR HEMSTOCK: She's crust enough on her

BAKER: Oh, I like 'em a bit brown. Good morning, everybody.

He swings up his basket and follows MRS SMALLEY out.

NURSE: How shameful to make a disturbance like that!

MR HEMSTOCK: We never have a bit of peace. She won't do a hand's turn in the house, and seems as if she can't bear herself because we manage without her.

HARRY: She's after the money.

NURSE: How dreadful! You are a strange family.

She goes into the parlour again, and keeps coming in and out with water ewer and so on. MR HEMSTOCK flourishes his balls of dough. HARRY puts on the saucepan.

MR HEMSTOCK: Dost think Job Arthur will marry our Susy?

HARRY: No.

MR HEMSTOCK: He seems to hang round her a good bit. Your mother often says he lets his bread get stale stoppin' there.

HARRY: If 'e married 'er, 'e'll settle her.

MR HEMSTOCK: Yes, he's all there.

HARRY: All but what he's short to pay his debts.

He goes out.

NURSE: I think I've done everything, Mr Hemstock.

She begins packing her black bag.

MR HEMSTOCK: Could you wait half a minute while I go to Goddard's?

NURSE: Well, ten minutes.

The old man takes a jar from the cupboard, and puts on his hat. At the door he meets the doctor, a clean-shaven fair man rather full at the stomach and low at the chest.

DR FOULES: Good morning, Mr Hemstock, you are going out?

MR HEMSTOCK: For a second, Doctor, just to the shop.

DR FOULES: I see. Then shall I go in?

MR HEMSTOCK: Oh, yes, Doctor.

DR FOULES: Thank you.

He enters. NURSE is just putting on her bonnet. The doctor stands confused.

NURSE (low and purring): Good morning.

DR FOULES: Nurse Broadbanks!

NURSE (low): Yes, just fancy.

DR FOULES: Well. I am surprised. Who ever

NURSE: I knew it was you. No other doctor would have been so polite about entering the house.

DR FOULES: Well, I can hardly find words, I am sure

NURSE: Fancy your keeping your old shyness.

DR FOULES (flushing): I don't know that I do

NURSE: I should have thought it would have worn off, all the experience you have had.

DR FOULES: Have I had so much experience?

NURSE: Eight years.

DR FOULES: Ah, Nurse, we don't measure experience by years.

NURSE: Surely, you have a quotation!

DR FOULES (smiling): No, I have not, for a wonder. Indeed I'm growing out of touch with literature.

NURSE: I shall not know you. You used to be

DR FOULES: Vox, et præterea nihil. "A voice, and nothing more."

NURSE: You are yourself. But you have not had much experience, in eight years?

DR FOULES: Not much has happened to me.

NURSE: And you a doctor!

DR FOULES: And I a doctor!

NURSE: But you have lost your old æsthetic look, wistful, I nearly said.

DR FOULES: Damnosa quid non imminuit dies? "Whom has not pernicious time impaired?"

NURSE: Not your stock of learning, evidently.

DR FOULES (bowing): Nor your wit, Nurse. Suum cuique. You have not?

NURSE: What?

DR FOULES: You have not married?

NURSE: Nurse Broadbanks.

DR FOULES: Of course, ha ha, how slow of me. Verbum sat sapienti.

NURSE: And you?

DR FOULES: What, Nurse?

NURSE: Married?

DR FOULES: No, Nurse, I am not. Nor, if it is anything to your satisfaction, likely to be.

NURSE: Your mother is still alive?

DR FOULES (bowing): Rem acu tetigisti. "You have pricked the point with your needle."

NURSE: I beg your pardon.

DR FOULES: Do not, I beg, do not.

NURSE: Semper idem, I know so much Latin.

DR FOULES: In what am I always the same, Nurse?

NURSE: Well, your politeness.

DR FOULES: Suaviter in modo, fortiter in re. My old motto, you remember.

NURSE: I do not know the English for it.

DR FOULES: "Gentle in manner, resolute in deed."

NURSE: In what deed, may I ask, Doctor?

DR FOULES: You may ask, Nurse. I am afraid I cannot tell you. And I, may I ask what you have done?

NURSE: Worked enough to be rather tired, Doctor, and found the world full of friends.

DR FOULES: Non multa sed multum. "Not many things, but much," Nurse. I could not say so much.

NURSE (laughing): No?

DR FOULES: Quid rides? "Wherefore do you laugh?"

NURSE: She lives with you here?

DR FOULES: My mother? Yes.

NURSE: It will always be said of you "He was a good son."

DR FOULES: I hope so, Nurse.

NURSE: Yes, it is the best.

DR FOULES (softly): You look sad.

NURSE: Not on my own behalf, Doctor.

DR FOULES: On mine, Nurse?

NURSE (reluctantly): No, not quite that.

DR FOULES: Tædium vitæ, all unresolved emotions and sicknesses go under that "weariness of life".

NURSE: Life? Doctor, do we get enough life to be weary of it? Work, perhaps.

DR FOULES: It may be, but

NURSE: You don't want life.

DR FOULES (smiling): Not much. I see too much of it to want it.

NURSE: Your mother will, I hope, live long enough to save you from experience.

DR FOULES: I hope it is a good wish, Nurse.

NURSE: Do you doubt it?

DR FOULES: Will you come and see us, Nurse?

NURSE: And see your mother?

DR FOULES: And see my mother, Nurse. (He bows.)

NURSE (smiling): Thank you, I will.

Enter HARRY, he stands rather confused in the doorway.

DR FOULES: Good morning, Mr Hemstock. How is Mrs Hemstock this morning?

HARRY: 'Er's pretty middlin', I believe.

Enter MR HEMSTOCK.

DR FOULES: I have just discovered that Nurse and I are old friends.

MR HEMSTOCK: I am glad of that

DR FOULES: Thank you.

NURSE: Dr Foules used to be my sweetheart.

MR HEMSTOCK: You don't mean it!

DR FOULES: Is it so long ago, Nurse, that you jest about it?

NURSE: I do not jest, Doctor. You are always to be taken very seriously.

DR FOULES (bowing): Thank you.

NURSE (to HARRY): Where did I leave my galoshes, Mr Hemstock?

HARRY: I'll fetch 'em.

He brings them in.

NURSE: How good of you to clean them for me!

They all stand watching while NURSE pulls them on.

DR FOULES: "A world full of friends," Nurse.

NURSE: Mr Hemstock and I are very good friends, are we not, Mr Hemstock?

HARRY: I dinna know, you know best, 'appen we are.

DR FOULES: You are repudiated, Nurse.

NURSE: Twice! You shouldn't have begun it.

DR FOULES: I am very sorry. It is never too late to mend.

NURSE: We've heard that before this morning. I must go.

DR FOULES: You will come and see us soon.

NURSE: I am at your disposal, Doctor. Good day, everybody.

ALL: Good day, Nurse.

DR FOULES: Well, I will see how Mrs Hemstock is.

He goes out.

MR HEMSTOCK: He's a nice fellow.

HARRY: Hm!

MR HEMSTOCK: Fancy he used ter court Nurse! I shouldna be surprised if they got together again.

HARRY: It doesna matter to me whether 'er does or not.

MR HEMSTOCK: No, it na matters to us, on'y I should like to see her settled wi' a decent chap. She's a good woman for any man. If I'd a been thy age

HARRY: Wi' that other hangin' round, an' no work to do, tha's ha' done wonders.

MR HEMSTOCK: T'other, tha's gin 'er the sack, an' tha can get work elsewhere.

HARRY: Dost think 'er'd ha'e me! (He laughs contemptuously.)

There is a noise of yelping and crying. The men stand and listen.

MR HEMSTOCK: It's that dog! An' Nurse!

HARRY rushes out. There is a great yelping and ki-yi-ing, a scream from NURSE. Immediately NURSE enters, carrying Patty, who flaps in a torn and gory state. HARRY follows. NURSE, panting, sets down Patty.

MR HEMSTOCK: Whatever

HARRY (flushing in fury): Has it hurt thee, did it touch thee?

NURSE: Me!

HARRY: I'll break its neck.

NURSE: Oh, don't be

HARRY: Where did it touch thee? There's blood on thee.

NURSE: It's not me, it's Patty.

HARRY: 'Appen tha non knows, 'appen it catched thee. Look at thy arm, look there!

NURSE: No, I'm not hurt, I'm sure I'm not.

HARRY: I'll break its neck, the brute.

NURSE: It had got hold of poor Patty by the wing, poor old bird.

HARRY: Look at thy cuffs. I'll break its neck.

NURSE: No, oh no, don't go out, no, get me some warm water, will you, and I'll see to Patty.

HARRY brings a bowl of warm water. NURSE takes bandaging from her bag.

MR HEMSTOCK: It's been at her before.

NURSE (to HARRY): You look after her other wing, keep her still, poor old bird (She proceeds to dress the wounded wing.)

MR HEMSTOCK: She'd be alright, Nurse, without you bothering.

NURSE: The idea, poor old thing!

MR HEMSTOCK: We've been many time worse hurt at pit, an' not half that attention.

NURSE: But, you see, you're not geese.

HARRY: We're not of as much count.

NURSE: Hand me the scissors, please, you don't know what you are

DR FOULES enters and stands in doorway.

MR HEMSTOCK: I keep telling him, if he set more stock by himself other folks 'ud think better of him.

NURSE: They might know him a little better if he'd let them.

DR FOULES: I see my help is superfluous.

NURSE: Yes, Doctor, it's one of the lower animals.

DR FOULES: Ah

CURTAIN

ACT II

SCENE I

The same evening. The HEMSTOCKS' kitchen, with the lamp lighted. The BAKER and HARRY sit with glasses of whisky.

BAKER: An' tha doesn't want 'er?

HARRY: I heave at the sight of her.

BAKER: She'll ha'e a bit o' money, I reckon.

HARRY: She's got to wait till old Hezekiah cops out, first.

BAKER: Hm! That'll be a long time yet, if he doesn't get married again. They say he's hankerin' after Nurse.

HARRY: 'Er'll niver ha'e 'im.

BAKER: Too old. But what hast got against Rachel?

HARRY: Nowt, but I heave wi' sickness at the thought of 'er.

BAKER: Hm! I like one as'll give as much as she takes.

HARRY: Sight more.

BAKER: It depends who's who.

HARRY: I can never make out why she went in service at the vicarage.

BAKER: Can't you? I've had many a nice evening up there. Baron an' Baroness go to bed at nine o'clock and then, Oh, all the girls know the advantage of being at the vicarage.

HARRY: Oh, an' does she ha'e thee up in the kitchen?

BAKER: Does she not half.

HARRY: I thought she wor so much struck on me!

BAKER: You wait a minute. If she can't feed i' th' paddock she'll feed at th' roadside. Not but what she's all right, you know.

HARRY: I do know.

BAKER: She's not got the spirit of your Susy. By Jove, she's a terror. No liberties there.

HARRY: Not likely.

BAKER: They say Bill left 'er in debt.

HARRY: He did.

BAKER: Hm! She'll have a long pull, then, to get it paid off.

HARRY: She's a-waitin' for my mother's money.

BAKER: Is she likely to get much?

HARRY: Happen a couple o' hundred, happen nowt.

BAKER: Depends on the will?

HARRY: Yes.

BAKER: A couple of hundred. . . .

HARRY: About that apiece, we should ha'e.

BAKER: Hm! You've seen the will?

HARRY: No, my mother takes good care o' that.

BAKER: Then none of you know? But you've some idea.

HARRY: We hanna. My mother's funny, there's no tellin' what 'er might do.

BAKER: Hm! She might leave the money away from her own children?

HARRY: I shouldna be a bit surprised.

BAKER: Hm! An' your Susy

MRS SMALLEY (entering): What about your Susy?

BAKER: Hello!

MRS SMALLEY: You're stoppin' a precious long time. Where might you be bound to-night?

BAKER: Not far.

MRS SMALLEY: No further than the vicarage, an' that's two closes off. But Rachel'll be givin' you up.

BAKER: 'Appen so.

MRS SMALLEY: Then she'll be tryin' her chances down here.

BAKER: I wish her luck.

HARRY (going out): I'll go an' get a bit o' bacca.

MRS SMALLEY: An' what do you call luck?

BAKER: Which do you reckon is a lucky-bag, me or your Harry?

MRS SMALLEY: You're both about as good: he's only got a little bunged-up whistle in him, an' many a hand's ferreted in you an' fetched out what's worth havin'.

BAKER: So I'm not worth havin'?

MRS SMALLEY: No, you're not, that's flat.

BAKER: So you wouldn't have me?

MRS SMALLEY: You're giving yourself away, are you?

BAKER (incisively): No, I'm not.

MRS SMALLEY: Indeed. And what's your figure, may I ask?

BAKER: A couple of hundred, to you; to anyone else, more.

MRS SMALLEY: Thank you for the offer, very kind of you, I'm sure. And how much is it to Rachel?

BAKER: Two hundred an' fifty.

MRS SMALLEY: Oh! So I'm worth fifty pound to you, am I, after I've put my two hundred down. Ready money?

BAKER: Six months bill.

MRS SMALLEY: You are a swine.

BAKER: Do you accept?

MRS SMALLEY: You are a pig! You'd eat cinders if you could get nowt else.

BAKER: I should. I'd rather have you than any of the boiling; but I must, I must, have

MRS SMALLEY: Two hundred?

BAKER: Not less.

MRS SMALLEY: Six months bill.

BAKER: Six months bill.

MRS SMALLEY: I hope you'll get it.

BAKER: I intend to.

MRS SMALLEY (after a speechless moment): You are a devil when you've had a drop.

BAKER: Am I a dear one?

MRS SMALLEY: Do you call yourself cheap?

BAKER: What do you think? I was always one of the "take it or leave it" sellers.

MRS SMALLEY: I think you imagine yourself worth a great sight more than you are.

BAKER: Hm! I should have thought you'd have found the figure easy. And I've always said I'd rather it was you than anybody.

MRS SMALLEY: You was mighty slow, then, once on a day.

BAKER: I was a young cock-sparrow then, common, but wouldn't die in a cage.

MRS SMALLEY: An' what do you reckon you are now?

BAKER: I'm an old duck that knows "dilly-dilly"!

MRS SMALLEY: "Come and be killed."

BAKER: Scatter me a bit of golden corn, two hundred, and you may wring my neck.

MRS SMALLEY: You must have an empty crop.

BAKER: A few pebbles that'll digest me if I don't

MRS SMALLEY: Debts?

BAKER: I said pebbles.

MRS SMALLEY: You're a positive fiend in drink.

BAKER: But what about?

Enter RACHEL, a tall, pale girl, with dark circles under her eyes. She has a consumed look, as if her quiet pallor smothered a fire. She wears a servant's cap and apron covered by a large dark shawl. She enters softly.

RACHEL: I thought I heard you two.

MRS SMALLEY (startled): You might knock!

RACHEL: Were you talking secrets?

BAKER: Have you come to look for me, Rachel?

RACHEL (cuttingly): You think a mighty lot of yourself.

BAKER: Have a drop of Scotch? No? How's that? There's Harry's glass, drink out of that.

RACHEL: You're very clever at giving away what's not your own. Give me yours.

BAKER: I've not finished with it, but you can drink with me. Here!

RACHEL: No, thank you.

BAKER (softly, smiling): Why, what has offended you?

RACHEL: Nothing, indeed.

BAKER: That's alright. I don't like you to be offended. As a sign of good luck. (She sips.) Thanks. I'm sorry I'm late.

RACHEL: You're not there yet, so you can't be late.

BAKER: Yes, I am there. What farther have I to go?

RACHEL (singing):

"You've got a long way to go,
You've got a long way to go,"

MRS SMALLEY (singing in a masculine voice):

"Before you get hold of the donkey's tether
You've got a long way to go."

BAKER (singing in a fine bass):

"If I had an ass and he wouldn't go,
Would I wallop him? Oh, dear no!
I'd give him some corn and say 'Gee whow,
Neddy, stand still while I mount, oh ho!'"

MRS SMALLEY: He's the donkey.

BAKER: Who doesn't make an ass of himself sometimes?

MRS SMALLEY: And we've got to give him some corn.

BAKER: For you'll never catch him to get hold of his tail, salt's no good.

MRS SMALLEY: How much corn? Tell her.

BAKER: Two hundred and fifty golden grains. No more.

RACHEL: What's up with him to-night?

MRS SMALLEY: Oh, he's had a drop, an' it always sets him on edge. He's like a razor. When he's had a drop, if you stroke him you cut yourself a-two.

RACHEL: Goodness!

BAKER: Rachel, I'd sell my immortal soul for two hundred and fifty golden sovereigns.

RACHEL: I'm not buying immortal souls, thanks.

BAKER: With this (He spreads out his hands.) this paper and string to wrap it in.

RACHEL: An' a nice parcel of goods you are!

BAKER: I'm a lucky bag, Rachel. You don't know all that's in me, yet.

RACHEL: And what is that, pray?

BAKER: I don't know myself. But you shall have leave to rummage me. (He throws open his arms.) Look! (He rises from his chair, as it were superbly. He is a fine, portly, not unhandsome man. He strikes a "superb" attitude.) Look, Rachel. For two hundred and fifty pounds, three months bill, I am (He bows.) your slave. You shall (He speaks with cynical sincerity.) bring down my head as low as you like (He bows low.), I swear it, and I never swore a lie.

RACHEL: But what do you want two hundred and fifty pounds for?

HARRY (entering): Has Nurse come?

BAKER: Not yet. Are you going to finish your glass? It has taken me all my time to stop the women sipping from it.

RACHEL: Story! You know I wouldn't

BAKER: Hush! Don't be rash now, or you'll hate me to-morrow.

RACHEL: And should you care?

BAKER: I am willing to give you full rights over my immortal soul and this paper and string

MRS SMALLEY: For two hundred down

BAKER (bowing, then looking to RACHEL): And fifty, Mrs Smalley.

RACHEL: What do you think of it, Susy? Is it a bargain?

BAKER (setting his cap on the back of his head and pulling on a large overcoat, he is well dressed): We have not struck hands yet.

MRS SMALLEY (to RACHEL): What do you say?

RACHEL: Nay, I want to hear what you say.

MRS SMALLEY: I'm going to say nowt, yet a while

RACHEL: Well, we'll see. (She pulls her shawl over her head to follow him.)

BAKER: Nay, I'm going down Northrop on business.

RACHEL: Wasn't you coming up?

BAKER: To the vicarage? I had this to tell you; that is all.

RACHEL: Well, I must say, but come up just for

BAKER: Not for a moment, Rachel. I am going down Northrop.

MRS SMALLEY: It's no good you saying nothing, Rachel. You might as well save your breath.

BAKER (smiling to RACHEL): You hear? I'll see you in the morning. Good night all.

Exit BAKER.

RACHEL (looking after him): I hate him.

MRS SMALLEY: I'm going home.

She hurries out. There is an awkward pause. HARRY sits bending over the fire.

RACHEL: How is your mother?

HARRY: Same.

RACHEL: Who's with her?

HARRY: Dad.

RACHEL: Where's Patty?

HARRY: Cupboard.

RACHEL: When do you expect Nurse?

HARRY: Dunno.

RACHEL: Have you been drinking whisky? (No answer.) Are you going to leave these glasses for Nurse to see? (No answer.) Are you going to let her see you drinking? (No answer.) Well, I do reckon you might speak to a body. I've not spoke to you for a week, hardly seen you. I can see you in your garden from the vicarage front bedrooms. I often watch you. Do you want your glass?

HARRY: Gi'e's it here!

RACHEL: You might say thank you. Job Arthur Bowers wants me to marry him. And I shouldn't be surprised if I did. (She cries.)

HARRY: Well, tha nedna scraight.

RACHEL: No, I mun only cry when I'm by myself. (Sobs.) I'm sure I'm sobbing half the night. (She cries.) Do you sleep bad? You do get up early, I can see your candle at half-past three, and you don't know how it frightens me.

HARRY: What's it frighten thee for?

RACHEL: I don't know. I feel frightened, for you seem so funny nowadays.

HARRY: 'As ter on'y just foun' it out?

RACHEL: You know I've told you about it many a time.

HARRY: A sight too often.

RACHEL: You are horrid. What have I done? Tell me.

HARRY: I'm non goin' to be made shift of. Tha'rt non goin' ter ma'e a spitton of me, ter spit the taste of somebody else out of thy mouth into.

RACHEL: Well, if I've been hateful, you've drove me to it, haven't you?

HARRY: I've told thee, I dunna want thee.

RACHEL: An' I went into service, so's I'd have something to do, an' so's I should be near, when

HARRY: Go on, an' so's, an' so's an' so's, I'm thy spitton, tha can spit owt inter me.

RACHEL: You're right, you're full o' sawdust.

HARRY (showing his teeth): What?

RACHEL: Sawdust, like a dummy. You've no more life in you.

HARRY (in a passion): What! What!

RACHEL: Sawdust.

HARRY (springing and seizing her by the shoulders): I'll settle thee!

RACHEL: You've been drinking.

HARRY (shouting): I'll settle thee, if I hang for it!

RACHEL: You're hurting me!

HARRY (quietly): Come here. (He binds her in her large shawl.)

RACHEL: Oh! What are you doing?

HARRY: I'll ha'e thee now, I will. (He seats her in the big armchair, strapping her with a leather belt he takes from his waist.)

RACHEL (quietly): Have you gone mad?

HARRY: Now then, answer me! Did ter court Bill Naylor a' the time as thou wert goin' wi' me?

RACHEL: No.

HARRY (his fist close to her eyes, loudly): Trewth!

RACHEL: Yes.

HARRY: Did ter tell him I used ter shout out that somebody wor coming if thou wanted to kiss me?

RACHEL: Yes.

HARRY: An' as I was allers swallerin' my spittle for fright?

RACHEL: Yes.

HARRY: An' I wor like a girl, as dursn't look thee atween the eyes, for all I was worth?

RACHEL: Yes.

HARRY: An' dursn't I?

RACHEL: Yes, an' don't. (She closes her eyes.)

HARRY: What! An' all t'other things about me as the pit was full of?

RACHEL: Oh, no! Oh, no!

HARRY: Yes, tha did!

RACHEL: No, oh no, Harry!

HARRY: An' are ter courtin' Job Arthur Bowers?

RACHEL: Oh!

HARRY: Scream, an' I'll squeeze thy head again' that chair-back till it cracks like a nut.

RACHEL (whimpering): Oh dear, oh dear.

HARRY: It is "oh dear", an' it 'as been for me "oh dear". Listen 'ere, tha brazend hussy. Tha keeps thy face shut when tha comes near me. Dost hear?

RACHEL: Yes.

HARRY: None o' thy cheek, not another word, in future, or I'll what?

RACHEL: No.

HARRY: An' dunna touch me till tha'rt axed. Not so much as wi' thy frock. Dost hear?

RACHEL: Yes.

HARRY: What dost hear?

RACHEL: I mustn't touch you.

HARRY: Not till thou'rt axed. An' lu' thee here, my lady, I s'll brain thee if tha says a word to me, sithee? (He thrusts his fist in her face.)

RACHEL: Somebody will come, let me go, let me go!

HARRY: An' what I've said, I mean, drunk or sover. Sithee?

RACHEL: Yes, Harry! Oh, let me go.

HARRY: I'll let thee go. (He does so, slowly.) An' tha can go wi' who tha likes, an' marry who tha likes, but if tha says a word about me, I'll come for thee. There! (He unbinds her. She lays her hand on his sleeve.) No! (He shakes her off. She rises and stands dejectedly before him.) I hate thee now enough to strangle thee.

RACHEL (bursting into tears): Oh, you are

HARRY: Now go wi' who tha likes, get off.

RACHEL: You are

HARRY: I want none o' thee, go!

She is departing.

An' ta'e thy shawl wi' thee.

She, weeping, picks up her shawl.

An' lap it round thee, it's a raw night.

She does so. He speaks gently now.

Now go.

Exit RACHEL. HARRY pours himself another glass of whisky. He goes to the cupboard.

Patty! Pat!

He puts his face caressingly among the bird's feathers.

We'll settle her Pat, eh? We'll stop her gallop. Hey, Pat!

He tosses the bird into the air wildly.

CURTAIN

A few moments later. The road just outside the HEMSTOCKS'. Deep darkness: two cottage lights in the background. In the foreground, a large white swing gate leading from the farmyard into the road, a stile beside the gate. MRS SMALLEY leans against the big white gatepost. Enter RACHEL, drying her tears, from the background. She steps through the stile. SUSY moves.

RACHEL: Oh! Oh! Oh Harry!

MRS SMALLEY: It's only me; shut up.

RACHEL: Oh, you did give me a turn, Susy!

MRS SMALLEY: Whatever's up?

RACHEL: Nothing. Who are you looking for?

MRS SMALLEY: Nobody.

RACHEL: Has Job Arthur gone?

MRS SMALLEY: You saw him go.

RACHEL: Not that I care.

MRS SMALLEY: I bet you don't. You carry on as if you don't care. You do. You needn't pretend to be so mighty struck on our Harry, you know it's all sham.

RACHEL: It's not, Susy. There's no sham about it; I wish there was. He's got his eye on Nurse, it's my belief.

MRS SMALLEY: An' she's got her eye on my mother's money, I know. She's sniffing like a cat over a mouse hole, an' cottoning on to our Harry.

RACHEL: She's deep, she is, an' he'd be as big as a lord for at the bottom he's that stuck-up he doesn't know what to do with himself.

MRS SMALLEY: I believe she knows something about the will.

RACHEL: Well, surely

MRS SMALLEY: An' from summat as my mother let drop, I'd be bound she's in it, wi' our Harry.

RACHEL: His mother always made me cheap in his eyes.

MRS SMALLEY: If I could get to know

RACHEL: Doesn't your Harry know?

MRS SMALLEY: How should I know what he knows?

RACHEL: My father's pining for Nurse, the old fool. I wish he'd get her. His money might get her. I'll buck him up.

MRS SMALLEY: I'll get in her way wi' our Harry as much as I can.

RACHEL: Alright. You are a bit gone on Job Arthur, aren't you?

MRS SMALLEY: He should ha' married me, by rights, twelve years back.

RACHEL: There's something fascinating about him. Does he really want £250?

MRS SMALLEY: Yes.

RACHEL: I believe my father would give it me, if I got married to please him.

MRS SMALLEY: Alright, there's your chance then.

RACHEL: You needn't be nasty, Susy. I don't want the chance.

MRS SMALLEY: You dodge round too many corners, like a ferret, you do.

RACHEL: At any rate, I'm not waiting for somebody to die and leave me bait to chuck to a fat fist of a fellow.

MRS SMALLEY: You'd better mind what you're saying, Rachel Wilcox.

RACHEL: I don't care about you. So there.

MRS SMALLEY: Doesn't 'er though? What about our Harry? I'll let him know a thing or two.

RACHEL: It's you as has been saying things, I know. You've been telling him about Job Arthur Bowers.

MRS SMALLEY: Oh, have I? You're mighty clever.

RACHEL: You don't need to be clever to see through you. But I'll make you pay for it, my lady.

MRS SMALLEY: What? Come out here

RACHEL: There's the Baron, an' they don't know I'm out!

She runs into hiding as a lantern appears down the lane. SUSY draws after her.

SUSY: What's he after?

RACHEL: Lovers. They hunt 'em out every Monday night. Shut up now. (In a whisper.) Does my white apron show?

BARON: We haf done good work this night.

BARONESS (tall and spare, in an antique cloak and bonnet): Seven couples, Baron, and we have only been out an hour. Isn't it terrible!

BARON: These miners are not men, they are animals that prowl by night.

BARONESS: The girls are worse, with their faces of brass. It is they who entice the young men into these naughty holes and crannies.

BARON: But if a man haf honour, will he not woo a maiden in her father's house, in the presence of her family?

BARONESS: This is a parish of sin, Baron, the people love sin.

BARON: Defiant in sin, they are! But I will overthrow them. I will drive them before me into the pit.

BARONESS: To think of that brazen besom telling us to go home and go to bed

BARON: And the man, ah, infamous, gross insult! And coward, to revile me that I have no child.

BARONESS: If they had a few less, and they born of sin, the low women! That is the house of the woman Hemstock. Have you seen her?

BARON: Not yet. I will not bury her, heathen and blasphemous woman. She shall not soil my graveyard of good dead. And those, her men folk, obstreperous and enemies of God, I will bow low their necks

BARONESS: Hush, there are some, I believe there are, behind the gate

BARON: More? Ah, misery, more than linked worms! Where? My dull eyes!

BARONESS: There, behind the gatepost

BARON (holding aloft the candle): Lovers, if you be there, why do you suck at sin? Is this honour, you man? There is no one there, Baroness.

BARONESS: Yes, Baron, yes. I can see her apron. Who are you? Come out of there. You, girl, I see you. Come out, for shame. You do not know what you are doing; or, if you do, you are the depth of wickedness. (A titter is heard.)

BARON: Where is the man? Show yourself, sir. Let me see the man. You lurk, sir, in a hole like a rat. Ah, the disgrace of mankind.

BARONESS: What is going to become of you, girl? Go home, before it is too late. Go home and learn to do your housework.

BARON: You press into the boughs of the trees, but the boughs are the little arms of God. You hide youselves deep in the darkness, which is but the pupil of the eye of God. Ah, like a hot spark you fret the eye of God with your lust.

BARONESS: You will rue it this time next year, I tell you.

BARON: The face of the man is full of shame, it is afraid lest it fall under my eye.

He holds the lantern peering at the woman. The BARONESS hovers close behind. RACHEL pushes SUSY out upon the little man. The lantern is extinguished.

BARONESS: Oh, oh, come away, Baron, come away!

BARON: Ha! Ha! (His voice is screaming.) It is the attack! Stand behind me, Baroness, I defend you. (He ends on a high note, flourishing a stick he carries.) I have hit him! Ha! Come on!

MRS SMALLEY: You've hit me, you little swine.

BARON: Stand behind me, Baroness. I defeat this man, I (He chokes with gutturals and consonants.)

MRS SMALLEY: Would you, you little swine!

BARON: I will thrash you, I will thrash you, low-bred knave, I will (He sputters into German.)

MRS SMALLEY: Let me get hold on thee, I'll crack thy little yed for thee.

BARONESS: Baron, Baron, they are murdering you!

BARON: Ah, my sword, my sword! Baroness, my sword! I keep him at bay with this stick.

MRS SMALLEY: I'll show thee, the little nuisance, whether tha'rt ter hit me on the shoulder.

BARON: I have not my strength of old, if I had my sword he were killed.

BARONESS: Thy are murdering the Baron! Help! Help! Oh Baron

RACHEL (suddenly rushing at her): Shut up, you old chuck! Shoo!

BARONESS (screaming): Baron! Rudolf, Rudolf! Oh-h!

BARON (groaning): Ah, Baroness!

He turns. SUSY rushes through his guard and seizes his wrist.

MRS SMALLEY: I'll have that stick!

BARON: The lady, the Baroness von Ruge, my wife, let me go to her!

MRS SMALLEY: Drop that stick, tha little!

BARON: Little, little again! Ah, my sword to thee. Let go my wrists, foul one, base one, fight thus! (He lapses into a foreign fizzle.)

BARONESS (fleeing): Help, help, help!

RACHEL (catching her by the end of her long cloak and pulling her round backwards): Whoa, you're going a bit too fast!

BARONESS: Whose voice is that? What? Oh-h!

Enter NURSE.

NURSE (breathless): Whatever is the matter? Who is it?

MRS SMALLEY: Drop that stick, little lizard

BARON: My wife! God, think of my wife!

BARONESS: Baron, they're killing me, Baron!

NURSE: Baroness! Oh, for shame, oh, how dreadful!

She runs to RACHEL, who flees.

HARRY (rushing up): What's goin' off?

NURSE: The poor Baron, an old man! Oh, how dreadful!

BARONESS: Rudolf, Rudolf! Where am I, what, where?

BARON: I will kill you.

HARRY (to his sister): Has ter no more sense, gre't hound?

MRS SMALLEY: What's tha got ter do wi' it? (to the BARON) Drop that stick!

BARON: I will certainly

HARRY: Come off! (He wrenches loose her wrists.)

BARON: Ha! (In triumph.) Thief! (He rushes forward. SUSY avoids him quickly. He attacks HARRY, fetching him a smart whack.)

HARRY: The little wasp

NURSE: Don't, Mr Hemstock, don't hurt him!

BARON: Ha! (He rushes again. HARRY dodges to avoid him, stumbles, the BARON gets in a blow. HARRY goes down.) Ha, I have smitten him, Ha!

BARONESS (fleeing): Baron, help! Help! Baron

BARON (pursuing): My wife

NURSE (to BARONESS): Come away, Baroness, come away quickly. The Baron is alright.

BARONESS: I have lost a galosher, he has lost his hat, and the lantern, oh!

BARON: Ah, Baroness, safe! God be glorified. What, oh, only Nurse. We haf been ambushed by a band of ruffians.

NURSE: You had better hurry to the vicarage, Baron, you will take cold.

BARON: Speak not to me of cold. We haf narrowly escaped. Are you wounded, Baroness?

BARONESS: Where is your hat, and the lantern, and my galosher?

BARON: What matter

NURSE: You had better take the Baroness home, Baron. She will be ill.

BARONESS: We can't afford to lose them, the lantern and your hat and a pair of galoshes.

BARON: Speak not of such

They leave.

HARRY (rising slowly): The little snipe!

MRS SMALLEY: It serves thee right.

CURTAIN

SCENE III

The kitchen of the HEMSTOCKS' house. MR HEMSTOCK is stirring a saucepan over the fire.

NURSE (entering): I am late. Are you making the food? I'm sorry.

MR HEMSTOCK: I hardly liked leavin' her, she's funny to-night. What's a' th' row been about?

NURSE: Somebody buffeting the Baron and Baroness. I've just seen them safely on the path. Has Harry come in?

MR HEMSTOCK: No, hark, here he is! Whatever!

The door opens. Enter HARRY, very muddy, blood running down his cheek.

Whatever 'as ter done to thysen?

HARRY: Fell down.

NURSE: Oh dear, how dreadful! Come and let me look! What a gash! I must bind it up. It is not serious.

MR HEMSTOCK: Tha'd better ta'e thy jacket off, afore Nurse touches thee.

HARRY does so. MR HEMSTOCK continues making the food. NURSE sets the kettle on the fire and gets a bowl.

NURSE (to HARRY): You feel faint, would you like to lie down?

HARRY: I'm a' right.

NURSE: Yes, you are all right, I think. Sit here. What a house of calamities! However did it happen?

HARRY: The Baron hit me, and I fell over the lantern.

NURSE: Dear me, how dreadful!

HARRY: I feel fair dizzy, Nurse, as soft as grease.

NURSE: You are sure to do.

Exit MR HEMSTOCK with basin.

HARRY: Drunk, like. Tha'rt as good as a mother to me, Nurse.

NURSE: Am I?

HARRY: My mother worna one ter handle you very tender. 'Er wor rough, not like thee.

NURSE: You see, she hadn't my practice.

HARRY: She 'adna thy hands. 'Er's rayther bad to-day, Nurse. I s'll be glad when 'er's gone. It ma'es yer feel as if you was screwed in a tight jacket, as if you'd burst innerds.

NURSE: I understand, it has been so long.

HARRY: It has. I feel as if I should burst. Tha has got a nice touch wi' thee, Nurse. 'Appen 'er'll leave me a bit of money

NURSE: Oh, Mr Hemstock!

HARRY: An' if I could get some work, dost think I ought to get married, Nurse?

NURSE: Certainly, when you've found the right woman.

HARRY: If I was in steady work, Nurse, dost think I'm a kid?

NURSE: No, why?

HARRY: I want motherin', Nurse. I feel as if I could scraight. I've been that worked-up this last eight month

NURSE: I know, it has been dreadful for you.

HARRY: I dunna want huggin' an' kissin', Nurse. I want, thar't a nurse, aren't ter?

NURSE: Yes, I'm a nurse.

HARRY: I s'll reckon I'm badly, an' then tha can nurse me.

NURSE: You are sick

HARRY: I am, Nurse, I'm heartsick of everything.

NURSE: I know you are

HARRY: An' after my mother's gone, what am I to do?

NURSE: What creatures you are, you men. You all live by a woman.

HARRY: I've lived by my mother. What am I to do, Nurse?

NURSE: You must get married

HARRY: If I was in steady work

NURSE: You'll get work, I'm sure.

HARRY: And if my mother leaves me some money

NURSE: I must tell you where the will is, for fear anything should happen.

HARRY: Then I can ax, is it done, Nurse?

NURSE: Just finished.

HARRY: Should I lie down?

NURSE: Let me straighten the sofa for you; don't get up yet. Then I must see to Mrs Hemstock, and I'll speak to you about the Baroness's things, and about the will, when I come back. How does the head feel?

HARRY: Swimming, like, like a puff o' steam wafflin'.

NURSE: Come along, come and lie down, there, I'll cover you up.

MR HEMSTOCK (entering): Is he badly?

NURSE: I think he'll be fairly by to-morrow.

MR HEMSTOCK: Tha'rt cading him a bit, Nurse.

NURSE: It is what will do him good, to be spoiled a while.

MR HEMSTOCK: 'Appen so, but it'll be a wonder.

NURSE: Why?

MR HEMSTOCK: Spoilin' is spoilin', Nurse, especially for a man.

NURSE: Oh, I don't know. How is Mrs Hemstock?

MR HEMSTOCK: Funny. I canna ma'e heads or tails of her.

CURTAIN

ACT III

SCENE I

The morning after the previous scene. The dining-room at the vicarage, a spacious but sparsely furnished apartment, the BARON considering himself in all circumstances a soldier. The BARON, in martial-looking smoking jacket, is seated at a desk, writing, saying the words aloud. The clock shows eleven. Enter BARONESS, in tight-sleeved paisley dressing-gown, ruched at neck and down the front. She wears a mobcap.

BARON (rising hastily and leading her to her chair): You are sure, Baroness, you are sufficiently recovered to do this?

BARONESS: I am only pinned together, Baron. I shall collapse if the least thing happens.

BARON: It shall not happen.

BARONESS: My head has threshed round like a windmill all night.

BARON: Did I sleep?

BARONESS: No, Baron, no, no! How do you find yourself this morning?

BARON: Younger, Baroness. I have heard the clash of battle.

BARONESS: I was so afraid you had felt it.

BARON: I, I, but I shall fall to no sickness. I shall receive the thrust when I am in the pulpit, I shall hear the cry, "Rudolf von Ruge"! I fling up my hand, and my spirit stands at attention before the Commander.

BARONESS: Oh Baron, don't. I shall dread Sunday.

BARON: Dread it, Baroness! Ah, when it comes, what glory! Baroness, I have fought obscurely. I have fought the small, inconspicuous fight, wounded with many little wounds of ignominy. But then, what glory!

BARONESS: Has Nurse come yet?

BARON: She has not, Baroness.

BARONESS: I wish she would.

BARON: You feel ill, hide nothing from me.

BARONESS: She promised to try and get the things. I know the hat will be ruined, but if we recover the galosh and the lantern, 'twill be a salvation.

BARON: 'Tis nothing.

BARONESS: 'Tis, Baron, your hat cost 15/- and my pair of galoshes, 3/6, and the lantern, 2/11. What is that, Baron? Reckon it up.

BARON: I cannot, I have not (a pause) it is twenty-one shillings and one penny.

BARONESS: 15/- and 3/6 15, 16, 17, 18m that's 18/6 and 2/11, 18, 19, 20. (Counting.) And five pence, Baron. Twenty-one shillings and five pence.

BARON: 'Tis nothing, Baroness.

BARONESS: 'Tis a great deal, Baron. Hark! Who is that called?

BARON: I cannot hear.

BARONESS: I will go and see.

BARON: No, Baroness, I go.

BARONESS: To the kitchen, Baron?

Exit. The BARON, at the window, cries on the Lord, in German.

NURSE (at the door): Good morning.

BARONESS (hastily turning back): Have you got them?

NURSE: The hat and the galosh, we couldn't find the lantern.

BARONESS: Those wicked Hemstocks have appropriated it.

NURSE: No, Baroness, I think not.

BARONESS: Your hat is not ruined, Baron, a miracle. Put it on, it looks as good as new. What a blessing. Just a little brushing, and my galosh is not hurt. But to think those wretches should secrete my lantern. I will show them

BARON: Baroness!

BARONESS: I was going to the kitchen. I hear a man's voice.

NURSE: The Baker's cart is there.

BARONESS: Ah! (Exit BARONESS.)

NURSE: I am very glad the Baroness is not ill this morning.

BARON: Ah Nurse, the villainy of this world. Believe that a number of miners, ruffians, should ambush and attack the Baroness and me, out of wrath at our good work. The power of evil is strong, Nurse.

NURSE: It is, Baron, I'm sorry to say.

BARON: I think those people Hemstock instigated this, Nurse.

NURSE: No, Baron, I am sure not.

BARON: Will you say why you are sure, Nurse?

NURSE: I saw, Baron. It was not Harry Hemstock, nor his father.

BARON: Then who, Nurse? They are criminals. It is wickedness to cover their sin. Then who, Nurse?

NURSE: Some people from Northrop. I cannot say whom. You know, Baron, you are an aristocrat, and these people hate you for it.

BARON: The mob issues from its lair like a plague of rats. Shall it put us down and devour the land? Ah, its appetite is base, each for his several stomach. You knew them, Nurse?

NURSE: No, Baron.

BARON: You heard them, what they said, their voices.

NURSE: I heard one say "Catch hold of Throttle-ha'penny!"

BARON: "Catch hold of Trottle-ha'penny", Throttle-ha'penny, what is that?

NURSE: I think it means the Baroness. They are so broad, these people, I can't understand them.

BARON: I will punish them. Under the sword they shall find wisdom.

BARONESS'S VOICE: Oh, shameless! Shameless!

RACHEL'S VOICE: He was looking at my brooch.

BARONESS'S VOICE: Come here, Baker, come back.

BAKER'S VOICE: A stale loaf to change, Baroness?

BARONESS'S VOICE: You shall go before the Baron this time. Go in the dining-room, Rachel.

BAKER'S VOICE: Me too?

Enter RACHEL, in cap and apron, the BAKER, and the BARONESS.

BAKER (entering): Thank you, Missis. Good morning, Nurse. Expect to find the Baroness in bed? I did.

BARONESS (to RACHEL): Stand there!

BARON (sternly to BAKER): Stand there! Take a seat, Nurse. Pray be seated, Baroness.

BAKER (seating himself in the armchair): Hope I haven't got your chair, Baron.

BARON: Stand, sir.

BAKER (to NURSE, as he rises): Nearly like my father said to the curate: "They're a' mine!"

BARON: Baroness!

BARONESS: He was, Baron, he was

RACHEL: He was bending down to look at my new brooch. (She shows it.)

BARONESS: With his arm

BAKER: On her apron strings

BARONESS: He was stooping

BAKER: To look at her new brooch.

BARON: Silence!

BARONESS: He kissed her.

BARON: Coward! Coward! Coward, sir!

BAKER: Ditto to you, Mister.

BARON: What! Sir! Do you know?

BAKER: That you are the "Baron von Ruge"? No, I've only your bare word for it.

NURSE: For shame, Mr Bowers.

BAKER: When a little old man, Nurse, calls a big young man a coward, he's presuming on his years and size to bully, and I say, a bully's a coward.

BARON: You contaminate my maid.

BAKER: I contaminate your maid?

BARONESS: The shameless baggage. What have I always said of her!

BARON: Baroness von Ruge! (to BAKER) You are going to marry her?

BAKER: It's a question generally put to the woman.

BARON: Answer me, sir.

BAKER: I couldn't say which she's going to marry, out of her one or two fellows.

BARONESS: Shameless! Ah, the slut!

BARON: I repeat, sir, do you intend to marry this maid?

BAKER: I hadn't fully made up my mind

BARON: Then, sir, you are a villain

BAKER: You've got the muscle of your years up, Mister

BARON: You threaten me!

BARONESS: Baron!

RACHEL: I sh'd have thought you'd more about you, Job Arthur Bowers.

NURSE (deprecating): Oh, Mr Bowers!

BAKER: Right you are, Nurse!

BARON: I say, sir, a man who kisses a maid

BAKER: Ought to be hanged for it, so say I.

BARON: Sir, your facetiousness is untimely. I say, a man who kisses a maid

BARONESS: Baron, such people do not understand

BARON (kissing her hand): Baroness!

RACHEL (melting): We're not given the chance.

BARON: Sir, is there no reverence in a kiss? If you strike a match against the box, even, you wonder at the outburst of fire. Then, sir, but do you wonder at nothing?

BAKER: Nothing's surprising, but everything is comical, Baron, that's how I find it.

BARON (puzzled and distressed): So! So! Ah, but a woman is, according to her image in the eye of the men.

BAKER (looking at the BARONESS): Some of us must have fancy eyes.

NURSE: How can you be so flippant?

BARONESS: A woman is what a man makes her.

BAKER: By gum, there's no tellin' what you might manufacture in time, then. It's a big job to begin of.

RACHEL (laughing): For shame, Job Arthur.

BARONESS: What have you to say? You bad creature! What wonder men are as they are?

BAKER: When the women make them.

BARON: You are of my parish?

BAKER: Yes, but I'm in Northrop Church choir.

BARON: You are a chorister? You wish to marry Rachel?

BAKER: As I say, I haven't decided.

BARON: But what are you doing? What of this maid?

BARONESS: What does he care! Are you a married man, Baker?

BAKER: Not that I know to, Missis.

BARON: Sir, I am an old man, you remind me

BAKER: Beg pardon, Baron.

BARON: And, a powerless, and I will say it, I will, a useless

BARONESS: Baron!

BARON: Sir, I shall soon be called in, and, sir, you are of my parish, Rachel is of my house. What have I done, who am responsible?

BAKER: Nay, Baron, I can't see as you're to fault.

BARON: My fault, sir, is failure, and failure without honour. In three campaigns, which are my life, I have been miserably beaten.

BARONESS: No, Baron, no. How are you to blame?

NURSE: No, Baron, you have not failed.

BARON: In Poland, in London, and in my parish of Greenway. Baroness, we retire to a cottage; I sit still and contain myself, under sentence, Baroness, your pardon!

BARONESS: You shall not retire, Baron. Before God, I witness, you are no failure. Ah, Rachel, see now what you've done.

RACHEL (weeping): It's not me.

BAKER: Nay, for that matter, would you marry me, Rachel, eh?

RACHEL: Opportunity's a fine thing, you mean.

BAKER: Will you marry me, Rachel?

RACHEL: I, yes, I will, Job Arthur.

BARON: She loves you, she let you kiss her. But you, sir, do you honour her?

BAKER: I do.

BARON: Then will you leave me?

BAKER: Good morning, sir, and thank you.

He and RACHEL leave.

BARONESS: You are not ill, Baron?

BARON: No, Baroness. Nurse, who is this man?

NURSE: The Baker? Oh, he's Job Arthur Bowers, a bit rackety. He lives down Greenhill with his old mother. She's as deaf as a post, and a little bit crazed. But she's very fond of her son.

BARON: Ah! She is mad? She is old? Will Rachel be good to her?

BARONESS: I very much doubt it.

NURSE: Rachel will be afraid of Job Arthur Bowers. He is too big for her ever to get her apron strings round him.

BARON (smiling slightly): I began to be afraid, Nurse

BARONESS (at the window): He is bringing my lantern.

NURSE: Who? Ah, that's right.

BARONESS: Will you ring, Baron? I will question that young man. We must get to the bottom of last night's affair, Baron.

BARON: Those ruffians shall not go unpunished. Still I have power for that.

BARONESS (to RACHEL): Show that young man in here. Nurse, you will help us. We must hold our own against these ungodly creatures. Must we not, Baron?

BARON: Ah, Baroness, still we fight.

RACHEL: Harry Hemstock.

HARRY (entering, his head bound up): I've brought this 'ere hurricane-lamp.

BARONESS: Thank you. And where did you find it?

HARRY: Where you'd lost it.

BARONESS: What have you done to your head?

HARRY (after a silence): You should know.

BARONESS: There, Baron. I was right. And you would have stolen the lantern if Nurse had not

BARON: Leave the lantern, Baroness. Sir, who were your accomplices in this nightly attack?

HARRY: What's 'e mean, Nurse?

NURSE: The Baron means what men were those that attacked the Baroness and him last night. I say they were some men out of Northrop, that you could not recognize them. Mr Hemstock came to your assistance, Baron.

BARON: Is that so?

HARRY: I pulled 'er off'n thee.

BARON: What is it he says, Nurse?

NURSE: He says he pulled the man away who was trying to hold you.

BARON: Ah! Tell me, sir, who was this ruffian?

HARRY: I non know, no.

BARON: Who struck you that blow? That you must know, and that must be told to me.

HARRY: Tha ought ter know thysen.

BARONESS: You are speaking to the Baron, remember.

HARRY: An't wor him as gin me a crack ower th' yed.

BARON: Then you were with the enemy. Now I behold you, sir. I will cause you, sir, I will make you to confess. I will see you punished. You shall suffer this course.

NURSE: You are mistaken, Baron.

BARON: Nurse, I will conduct this inquiry of myself. It is not of myself. But your cowardice, yours and those others', to attack a lady, by night. There is a penalty for such, sir; I say you are vile, and you shall name me the other villains.

HARRY: There was no other villains, without you call a couple of women villains.

BARON: What mean you by a couple of women?

BARONESS: He doesn't know what he is talking about.

NURSE: There were some men, Mr Hemstock, from Northrop.

HARRY: Well, if there wan, I didna see 'em. All I see'd was two women draggin' at th' old Baron.

BARON: You mean to say we were attacked only by two women, Baroness?

NURSE: He must be mistaken.

BARONESS: These people would say anything.

BARON: Tell me, sir, tell me the truth at once.

HARRY: I've told you the truth.

BARON: It was some men, Baroness? At least, Baroness, one man there was

BARONESS: There was one man, how many more I can't say.

BARON: The throat of these people is fuller of untruth than a bird's gizzard

HARRY: It is the truth I've told you.

BARON: Nurse, speak, was it two women?

NURSE: It certainly was men, Baron.

HARRY: Well, it certainly wan't, an' I'm not a liar.

BARON: Then it was two women?

HARRY: It was.

BARON: And a woman has smitten your head?

HARRY: No, you did that youself, with your thick stick, when I'd pulled our Susy off'n you. An' I fell over your lantern and it cut me.

BARONESS: A likely tale.

HARRY: Is it true, Nurse Broadbanks?

NURSE: I think you are mistaken, Mr Hemstock. Oh, do not be so persistent.

HARRY: I'll not be made a liar of. Wheer's Rachel?

BARONESS: Why Rachel? She has nothing to do with it.

HARRY: Fetch her in then.

NURSE: She has just been in. She is engaged to Job Arthur Bowers

HARRY: I don't care what she is.

BARON: I will ring.

BARONESS: Do not, Baron, do not trouble.

BARON: Sir, it was not two women, I defy you, sir. You make me a silly thing; it is your spleen.

BARONESS: You had better go, you.

HARRY: I'm not going to be made a liar of.

Enter RACHEL.

Rachel, who was it knocked the Baron's hat off an' shook him last night?

NURSE: Do you know the names of those men from Northrop, Rachel?

RACHEL: It wan't him, Baron, he helped you.

BARON: He would patch me with shame. You saw this attack?

RACHEL: I was just slipping down to get some milk from Mrs Smalley, there was none for supper

BARON: And what did you see?

RACHEL: I saw some men, an' I heard some shouting, and I saw somebody hit him on the head. Then I ran home, and I'd just got in when you came.

HARRY: Why, wan't it you and our Susy as was raggin' the Baron an' Baroness, an' I come up an' stopped you?

RACHEL: Me! Me an' your Susy?

HARRY: You shammer!

RACHEL: I know you went up an' stopped the men, whoever they was

HARRY: So I'm a liar? So I'm a liar?

BARONESS: Yes, and you may go.

HARRY: So I'm a liar, Nurse Broadbanks?

He goes out.

BARON: God help us, we begin to believe in the plots they imagine against us. (He looks at his hands.) It was not two women, Baroness?

BARONESS: No, Baron, no.

BARON: You saw several men, Nurse?

NURSE: Yes, Baron.

BARON: Rachel, but why weep! Rachel, he defended me against men?

RACHEL (sobbing): Yes, Baron.

BARONESS: Rachel, leave the room.

RACHEL leaves.

BARON: Nurse, I am a soldier.

NURSE: You are, Baron.

BARON: I must reward that, fellow, although

NURSE: It is good of you, Baron.

BARONESS: And you called yourself a failure, Rudolf.

BARON: I can, I must speak for him at the colliery. There I still have some influence.

NURSE: It is so good of you.

BARON: He has suffered already for his opposition. It is not good for the enemies of God to prosper. But I will write to my nephew.

NURSE: I could leave a letter, Baron, I am going past the colliery.

BARON: I will write now, then my honour is free. (Seats himself at the desk.) "My dear Nephew, I am placed under an obligation to that man of whom I have spoken to you before, Henry Hemstock, of the cottage at the end of the glebe close. It is within the bounds of your generosity to relieve me of this burden of gratitude contracted to one of such order. You will, of your fullness of spirit, lap over the confine of my debt with bounty. Your Aunt salutes you, and I reach you my right hand. Rudolf von Ruge." The manager of the collieries is as my own son to me, Nurse.

BARONESS: And he is a good son. He is my nephew.

NURSE: I will leave the letter.

CURTAIN

SCENE II

Evening of the same day. NURSE'S room, the sitting-room of a miner's cottage: comfortable, warm, pleasant. NURSE in the armchair on one side of the fire. MR WILCOX on the other. He is a stout, elderly miner, with grey round whiskers and a face like a spaniel.

MR WILCOX: No, Nurse, I've not a bit of comfort.

NURSE: Why shouldn't Rachel stay and look after you?

MR WILCOX: Nay, don't ask me, an ungrateful hussy. And I can't seem to get a housekeeper as'll manage for me.

NURSE: It is difficult.

MR WILCOX: I've been trying this last ten years, an' I've not had a good one yet. Either they eat you up, or waste, or drink. What do you think to-day? You know how it was raining. I got home from pit soaked. No breeches an' waistcoat put to warm, fire nearly out.

NURSE: Oh, it is too bad.

MR WILCOX: An' in the fender, a great row of roast potatoes, hard as nag-nails, not done a bit,

NURSE: What a shame

MR WILCOX: An' not a morsel of meat to eat to them. She'd aten the great piece of cold mutton left from yesterday, an' then said I hadn't left 'er no money for no meat.

NURSE: How stupid!

MR WILCOX: So it was taters, you had to chomp 'em like raw turnip, an' drippin', an' a bit of a batter puddin' tough as whit-leather.

NURSE: Poor man.

MR WILCOX: An' no fire, there never is when I come home. I believe she sells the coal.

NURSE: Isn't it dreadful?

MR WILCOX: An' they're all alike.

NURSE: I suppose they are.

MR WILCOX: They are. You know I'm an easy man to live with, Nurse.

NURSE: I'm sure you are.

MR WILCOX: One as gives very little trouble. Nay, I can fettle for myself, an' does so.

NURSE: I have seen you.

MR WILCOX: And I think I deserve a bit better treatment, Nurse.

NURSE: I'm sure you do.

MR WILCOX: An' I ought to be able to get it. If I was drunken or thriftless I should say nothing.

NURSE: But you're not.

MR WILCOX: No, I'm not. I've been a steady and careful man all my life. A Chapel-going man, whereas you're Church, but that's a detail.

NURSE: It ought not to matter.

MR WILCOX: You know, Nurse, I've got four good houses, lets at six shillings each.

NURSE: Yes, I know you have.

MR WILCOX: Besides a tidy bit in the bank.

NURSE: And you have saved it all?

MR WILCOX: Every penny.

NURSE: Ha!

MR WILCOX: An' there's on'y Rachel. I'd give her a couple of houses straight off, an' then we should be alright there: nobody could grumble.

NURSE: You could do that, of course.

MR WILCOX: Nurse, do you know how old I am?

NURSE: No, Mr Wilcox.

MR WILCOX: I'm just fifty-eight.

NURSE: Hm! I should have thought you were more.

MR WILCOX: I'm not.

NURSE: It is comparatively young.

MR WILCOX: It's not old, is it? And though I've been a widower these ten years, I'm not, I'm not good for nowt, d'yer see?

NURSE: Of course you're not.

MR WILCOX: An' you know, Nurse, you're just the one for me.

NURSE (laughing): Am I, Mr Wilcox?

MR WILCOX: Nurse, will you tell me your name?

NURSE: Broadbanks.

MR WILCOX: You know I meant your Christian name. Don't torment me, Nurse, I can't stand it.

NURSE: I was baptized Millicent Emily.

MR WILCOX: "Millicent Emily", it's like the "Song of Solomon". Can I say it again?

NURSE: If you will say it only to yourself.

MR WILCOX: My name is James, Jim for short.

NURSE: I thought it was Hezekiah, or Ezekiel.

MR WILCOX: Hezekiah's my second name, James Hezekiah.

NURSE: I like Hezekiah better.

MR WILCOX: Do you, I thought you didn't. Oh, I'm glad you like it. But yours is lovely.

NURSE: I prefer Nurse.

MR WILCOX: So do I, nice and short. (A pause.) Shall I sing to you, Nurse?

NURSE: Do you sing?

MR WILCOX: Oh, yes, I used to be a great one at "Ora pro Nobis". Should I sing you "Gentle Annie"? I used to sing that forty years since.

NURSE: When you were courting, Mr Wilcox?

MR WILCOX: Afore that.

He hesitates, goes to the piano and, after fumbling, begins to vamp to "What Are the Wild Waves Saying". He begins to sing, "lamentoso".

NURSE: There's someone at the door!

Not hearing, or observing, he continues to play. She opens to DR FOULES: they stand smiling. MR WILCOX stops playing and wheels round.

DR FOULES: "Music, when soft voices die, vibrates in the memory."

NURSE: Mr Wilcox was enlivening my leisure. Do you know Mr Wilcox, Dr Foules?

DR FOULES: I have not had the pleasure till now.

He bows.

MR WILCOX: Good even', I wasn't aware as anybody was here.

DR FOULES: "By rapture's blaze impelled he swelled the artless lay."

NURSE: I think Mr Wilcox sings very well indeed. Will you finish, Mr Wilcox?

MR WILCOX: No, thanks, I must be going.

DR FOULES: Pray do not let me hasten you away.

MR WILCOX: Oh, I was just going. Well, happen you'll call at our house, Nurse?

NURSE: I will, Mr Wilcox.

He leaves.

DR FOULES: Did I interrupt you?

NURSE: You did not interrupt me.

DR FOULES: Then I incur no disfavour?

NURSE: Not for stopping poor Mr Wilcox at "Brother, I hear no singing", Poor man!

DR FOULES: You pity him?

NURSE: I do.

DR FOULES: Ah! Is it of the mind-melting sort?

NURSE: I do not understand.

DR FOULES: "For pity melts the mind to love"

NURSE: No, poor man. I can just imagine my mother, if I took him down to Kent. Well, you've done a nice thing for yourself

DR FOULES: You daren't face family criticism?

NURSE: I daren't.

DR FOULES: Ah! Then he does aspire?

NURSE: Poor old fellow!

DR FOULES: I do not like your pity, Nurse, however near akin it may be to something better.

NURSE: You have often incurred it, Doctor.

DR FOULES: Which of the two, Nurse?

NURSE: The pity, of course. I have said "poor boy".

DR FOULES: Why?

NURSE: Why? (She laughs.) Because, I suppose, you were pitiable.

DR FOULES (blushing): You mean I was to be pitied. Why?

NURSE: Because you were not like the Pears' Soapy baby, "He won't be happy till he gets it," but you went on washing your self without soap, good as gold.

DR FOULES: I cannot apply your simile.

NURSE: Perhaps not. I never was literary.

DR FOULES: You have grown brilliant and caustic, if I may say so.

NURSE: It is the first time I have been accused of brilliance.

DR FOULES: Then perhaps I am the steel which sheds the sparks from your flint.

NURSE: Oh, the sparks may come, but they're not noticed. Perhaps you are only the literary man who catches them on his tinder and blows them into notice. You love a phrase beyond everything.

DR FOULES: Really, I hardly recognize you, Nurse.

NURSE: And what did your mother say of me?

DR FOULES: I thank you for calling so soon. Did she seem changed, to you?

NURSE: She looks very ill.

DR FOULES: Yes, I am worried.

NURSE: You are afraid it is something serious?

DR FOULES: Yes.

NURSE: I hope not. But it put me about to see her looking so frail. She was very kind to me.

DR FOULES: You are very good, Nurse.

NURSE: It is my duty to be sympathetic, Doctor.

DR FOULES: And use is second nature. I will take courage, Nurse.

NURSE: Will it not be a complete disguise?

DR FOULES: Your duty does not extend to me, Nurse.

NURSE: No, Doctor.

DR FOULES: You wish me to see you in your new guise, Nurse. You stick daw's feathers among your dove's plumage.

NURSE (laughing): What, am I a dove then? It is a silly bird.

DR FOULES: You have had a hard time, Nurse?

NURSE: I have got over the hardness, thank you. It is all moderate, now.

DR FOULES: Might it not be more than moderate?

NURSE: I hope it will be some day.

DR FOULES: Could I help it, do you think?

NURSE: Everybody helps it, by being amiable

DR FOULES: But might I not help it more particularly? You used to

NURSE: Say you are in love with me, Doctor

DR FOULES: I have always been

NURSE: Then the light has been under a bushel.

DR FOULES: "Blown to a core of ardour by the awful breath of -" (He smiles very confusedly.) I may hope then, Nurse.

NURSE (smiling): Along with Mr Wilcox.

DR FOULES: Thank you for the company.

NURSE: Look here, Arthur, you have lived like a smug little candle in a corner, with your mother to shelter you from every draught. Now you can get blown a bit. I do not feel inclined to shelter you for the rest of your life.

DR FOULES: Thank you.

NURSE: I am sorry if I am nasty. But I am angry with you.

DR FOULES: It is evident.

NURSE: And I will still come and see your mother, if I may. She is a woman to respect.

DR FOULES: I do not order my mother's comings and goings. The case is the reverse, you remember.

NURSE: Very well. On your high horse, you are more like the nursery than ever.

DR FOULES: Thank you.

NURSE (mimicking): Thank you.

DR FOULES: I am surprised

NURSE: I am surprised, but was that someone at the door?

DR FOULES: I could not tell you.

NURSE: Excuse me, I will see.

DR FOULES: Let me go, first. (Catching his hat to depart.)

NURSE (opening the door): You, Mr Hemstock. Will you come in?

Enter HARRY.

DR FOULES: Good evening, Mr Hemstock. I will make way for you.

NURSE: "Applications considered Tuesday, between seven and nine p.m." That is your meaning, Doctor?

DR FOULES: With your usual astuteness, you have it.

NURSE: With my usual astuteness, I have avoided so far the "Matrimonial Post". This is the irony of fate, Doctor. It never rains but it pours.

DR FOULES (bowing to NURSE and HARRY): The third time pays for all, they say.

NURSE (laughing): I will tell you to-morrow.

DR FOULES: It will not be too late to drop me a post card.

NURSE: I will see. Good night, Dr Foules.

DR FOULES: Good night, Nurse Broadbanks. I wish you luck.

NURSE: And lifelong happiness.

DR FOULES: Good night!

Exit DR FOULES.

NURSE: He is very pleasant, isn't he?

HARRY: They say so.

NURSE: How is Mrs Hemstock?

HARRY: She's worse. She's not speakin'.

NURSE: Oh, I'm sorry to hear that. Did you want me to do anything? Poor thing, it will be a relief when she's gone.

HARRY: The 'owd doctor's bin. He told us to ax you to see her settled down

NURSE: Shall I come now?

HARRY: Or in about half an hour's time, when you're ready.

NURSE: I may as well come now, when I've just tidied the room. Are you going to sit up with her?

HARRY: No, my father is, an' our Susy. I'm going to work.

NURSE: Going to work? I thought you hadn't a place.

HARRY: They sent me word as I wor to go to-morrow, buttyin' wi' Joe Birkin.

NURSE: And will it be a good place?

HARRY: Ha! It's a sight better than ever I expected.

NURSE: Oh, that is nice, isn't it?

HARRY: It's better nor mormin' about at home.

NURSE: It is. I'm so glad, Mr Hemstock. Then you'll stop at Greenway?

HARRY: I'm reckonin' so. There's nowt else, is there?

NURSE: No, why should there be? You'll have to begin afresh after Mrs Hemstock has gone

HARRY: I s'll make a start o' some sort.

NURSE: You will? Do you know, I've had old Mr Wilcox here tonight.

HARRY: Oh, ah?

NURSE: He's so comical. He was singing to me. (She laughs into her hand.)

HARRY: He must ha' wanted summat to do

NURSE: I think so. You never heard anything like it in your life.

HARRY: 'E never wor but dosy-baked.

NURSE (purring): What does that mean?

HARRY: Soft, batchy, sawney.

NURSE: Poor old chap. It's no use being angry with him, is it?

HARRY: What for?

NURSE: For thinking I would accept him.

HARRY: No, it's not good bein' mad wi' him.

NURSE: He looked so crestfallen.

HARRY: He'll be just as game by to-morrow.

NURSE: Of course he will. Men only pretend to be so heartbroken. By supper-time they've forgotten.

HARRY: An' what's a woman do?

NURSE: I don't know. You see it means more to a woman. It's her life. To a man it's only a pleasant change.

HARRY: To all appearances, you'd think it worn't such a life-an'-death affair to her.

NURSE: Why?

HARRY: Woman is reckoned to be pinin' for you, goes an' makes a liar an' a fool of you in front of other folks.

NURSE: You mean Rachel Wilcox.

HARRY: Ah, 'appen I do.

NURSE: But, poor old Baron, it would have killed him.

HARRY: Then let him die. What good is he, here or anywhere else?

NURSE: Oh, Mr Hemstock!

HARRY: Besides, she did it to spite me, because 'er wor mad wi' me.

NURSE: But she is engaged to Mr Bowers.

HARRY: 'Appen so. 'Er bites 'er nose off to spite her face.

NURSE: But poor old Baron, it would have been so cruel.

HARRY: Would he have stopped tellin' everybody else the truth?

NURSE: But you can't judge in that way

HARRY: Why canna I? You make a liar an' a swine of me, an' a dam' fool of him

NURSE: Oh, come, Mr Hemstock.

HARRY: He is a little fool, an' wants to boss everybody else wi' it, an' a'

NURSE: You ought not to speak of the Baron like that.

HARRY: No, it's all palaver, an' smooth talk. I'll see anybody in hell before I'm fed wi' mealy-mouthed words like a young pigeon.

NURSE: I think you don't know what you're talking about.

HARRY: Dunna I though, but I do. I'm not going to be made a convenience of, an' then buttered up, like a trussed fowl.

NURSE: There is no one wants to butter you up, to my knowledge.

HARRY: Alright, then, then there isn't.

NURSE: And all this, I think, has been very uncalled for and unnecessary.

HARRY: Alright, then, an' it has. But I'm not a kid, nor to be treated like one

NURSE: It's there you make your mistake.

HARRY: Nay, it's somebody else as had made a mistake.

NURSE: Yes, we do think the quiet vessels are the full ones. But it seems they only want shaking to rattle worse than any.

HARRY: Alright. Say what you like.

NURSE: Thank you, I don't wish to say any more, except that I pity whoever has you, for you seem to be in a state of chronic bad temper.

HARRY: Alright, I'll be going.

NURSE (who has been tidying the room): I will be at your house in ten minutes.

HARRY: There's no occasion to hurry, am I to wait for you?

NURSE: No, thank you, I would rather come alone.

CURTAIN

ACT IV

The evening after the last scene. It is the third day of the play. The kitchen at the HEMSTOCKS'.

NURSE: And what about the fire in the room?

SUSY: I'll let it go out and take the ashes up by daylight. It's falling dusk, an' I don't like being in by myself.

NURSE: Poor Mrs Hemstock, she went away quickly at the last.

SUSY (red-eyed, sniffing): She did that. Eh, but wan't she wasted? A fair skeleton! I'm glad you laid her out, Nurse.

NURSE: I shall miss her. I've been coming here over a year now.

SUSY: I hope I don't lie like that. She used to be as strong as a horse. But she was hard, you know.

NURSE: Perhaps she had enough to make her.

SUSY: She had, wi' my father an' the lads. She was easiest wi' our Harry. He was always mother's lad.

NURSE: Yet they have been so indifferent

SUSY: At the bottom they haven't. She never forgave him for going with Rachel Wilcox, an' he was always funny-tempered, would rool up like a pea-bug, at a word.

NURSE: I thought she favoured Rachel Wilcox.

SUSY: No, hated her; but she used her to make game of him.

NURSE: She is engaged to the Baker now.

SUSY: Yes. He's only having her for her money, an' she'll hate him when she's rubbed the fur off a bit. But she's one would fuss round a pair of breeches on a clothesline, rather than have no man.

NURSE: I don't like her.

SUSY: Not many does. She fair pines for our Harry, yet she'd have Job Arthur for fear of getting nobody.

NURSE: How dreadful! (She goes for her cloak.)

SUSY: Nay, dunna go. Stop an' ha'e a cup o' tea. I durstn't stop in by mysen. The kettle'll boil in a minute. (She lays the table.)

NURSE: I really ought to go.

SUSY: Don't, I should be scared to death. You'll stop five minutes, Nurse.

NURSE: A quarter of an hour.

SUSY (staring): What's that?

NURSE (going to the door): It's only Patty.

SUSY: She's been that lost a' day without our Harry.

NURSE: Poor old Patty!

Enter HARRY.

SUSY: Tha'rt a bit sooner than I thought fer.

HARRY (surly): Am I?

SUSY: I hanna been able to get thee no dinner.

HARRY: Why?

SUSY: She on'y died at two o'clock, an' we've been busy ever sin', haven't we, Nurse?

NURSE: We have, Mrs Smalley.

SUSY: Shall ter ha'e tea wi' me an' Nurse?

HARRY: No.

SUSY: What then?

HARRY: Nowt.

SUSY: Shall ter wesh thysen?

HARRY: Ha.

SUSY: Pump wor frozen this mornin'

HARRY: I know.

SUSY fetches a large red pancheon from outside, puts in cold water, brings towel and soap, setting all on a stool on hearth-rug. HARRY sets tin bottle and knotted snap-bag on table, takes off his cap, red wool scarf, coat, and waistcoat. He pours hot water from boiler into pancheon, strips off his singlet or vest, he wears no shirt, and kneels down to wash. NURSE and SUSY sit down to tea.

NURSE (to HARRY): You must be tired to-day. (No answer.)

SUSY: I bet his hands is sore, are they? (No answer.) Best leave him alone, they always grumble about their hands, first day.

HARRY: Wheer's my Dad?

SUSY: Gone to registrar's.

NURSE: Yes, they must take some time to harden.

SUSY: Shall you sit there, Nurse? I'd better light the lamp, you can't see.

HARRY: Tha nedna.

SUSY: What's thaigh to stop me for?

NURSE: No, I like the twilight, really.

SUSY: There's a lot o' dirt wi' a collier, an' mess.

NURSE: Yes.

SUSY: I allers said I'd not marry one. I'd had enough wi' my father an' th' lads.

NURSE: They say it's clean dirt.

SUSY: Is it? Muck an' mess, to my thinkin'.

NURSE: Yes, I suppose so. I used to think it would be dreadful.

SUSY: But you've altered.

NURSE: Well, I've thought about it, I'm afraid I should never fit in.

SUSY: No, you're too much of a lady, you like a lady's ways.

NURSE: I don't know. Perhaps one does get a bit finicky after a certain time.

SUSY (to HARRY): Dost want thy back doin'?

He grunts assent. She washes his back with a flannel, and wipes it as she talks.

NURSE: It's the thought of it day after day, day after day, it is rather appalling.

SUSY: The thought of any man, like that, is.

NURSE (smiling): It was not the man, it was the life, the company one would have to keep.

SUSY: Yes. So you wouldn't marry a collier, Nurse?

NURSE: Yes, I would, for all that. If I cared for him.

SUSY: That makes the difference.

NURSE: It does.

SUSY: I can't imagine you married to a collier.

NURSE: Sometimes it seems mad, to me; sometimes it doesn't.

SUSY: I shouldn't ha' thought, though, Nurse, you'd ha' had one

NURSE: No? I might.

SUSY: Not an old one?

NURSE: Certainly not an old one. Not Mr Wilcox.

SUSY: Ha. Have another cup? I wish Patty would keep still. She fair worrits me. I'm sure I'd like to drop your cup, she made me jump that much.

NURSE: I am surprised you are nervous.

SUSY: We all are. I wonder, Nurse, where my mother's will is?

NURSE: Oh, I meant to have told you. In the socket of the bedpost nearest the drawers, at the top.

SUSY: Would you believe it!

NURSE: She was very quaint sometimes. Poor Mrs Hemstock.

SUSY: Do you think she was in her right mind?

NURSE: Oh, yes, and Doctor does, too.

SUSY: Well, I used to have my doubts.

NURSE: Poor Mrs Hemstock.

A knock.

SUSY: Oh!

RACHEL (entering): I thought there was nobody in, seeing no light. Is Nurse here?

NURSE: Yes.

RACHEL: The Baroness wants you to go up, she's got a pain. I've been to your place for you.

NURSE: Poor Baroness! What is the matter?

RACHEL: She's got a pain in her shoulder.

NURSE: Rheumatism?

RACHEL: She says she believes it's pleurisy.

NURSE (smiling): Poor old Baroness; she does fancy.

RACHEL: But she won't pay for a doctor, fancy or no fancy, not if she can help it. Her fancy mustn't cost her anything.

NURSE: She knows I can treat her. I can go straight there.

RACHEL: Oh, an' will you go an' see what's up with my father? He's not been to work, been in bed all day, can't eat, won't have the doctor, fading away

NURSE: That is sad! What ails him?

RACHEL: I don't know, Minnie's been up for me. Says he feels hot inside, an' believes he's got an inflammation.

NURSE: I'll call if I have time. I must go.

RACHEL: He's done nothing but ask were his eyes bloodshot, and would Minnie be frightened if he turned delirious. She's frit, an' I can't go down

NURSE: I will call. Good night, everybody.

Exit NURSE.

SUSY: I must light the lamp.

RACHEL: I didn't hear till four o'clock as she'd gone. Was she unconscious?

SUSY: Yes, all day.

RACHEL (to HARRY, who is struggling into his shirt): And was you at work? Fancy, you been at home all this time, then it to happen the first day you was away. Things do happen cruel.

SUSY: Shall you give him his tea, while I go an' see to my lad?

RACHEL: I mustn't be long.

SUSY goes out.

What shall you have?

HARRY: Nowt.

RACHEL: Oh, you must 'ave somethink. Just a cup of tea, if nothing else. Come on, come an' sit here. See, it's waiting. You must be fair sinkin' after bein' at work all day. I've thought of you every minute, I'm sure. I've heard the driving engines shuddering every time, an' I've thought of you. (She cuts bread and toasts it.) They say you're hard, but they don't know. (Suspicion of tears.) I used to think myself as you was a kid, a frightened bit of a rabbit, but I know different now. (She cries.) I know what you've had to go through, an' I've been a cat to you, I have. I know what you've felt, as if you was pushed up against a wall, an' all the breath squeezed out of you, her dyin' by inches, an' I've been a cat to you. (She butters the toast.)

HARRY: Tha needna do that for me.

RACHEL: Yes, do eat a bit, you'll be sinkin'. I've had no tea, I'll eat a bit with you, if you will. (She sits down, drinks tea, and eats a little.) You know I've fair hated myself, I've wished I was dead. But I needn't talk about myself. Are your hands sore?

HARRY: A bit.

RACHEL: I knew they must be, because you've worked like a horse, I know you have, to stop thinking. I can see you're dog-tired. Let me look. (She takes his hand.) Fair raw! (Melting into tears.) You don't care a bit about yourself, you don't, an' it's not fair.

HARRY: Tha hasna bothered thysen above thy boot-tops.

RACHEL: I know I haven't. Oh, I was jealous of your mother, 'cause I knowed you was fonder of her

HARRY: Tha nedna (She weeps, he hides his face.)

RACHEL: I s'll never forgive myself

HARRY: Dunna

RACHEL, sobbing, goes to him, takes his head on her bosom, and rocks it.

RACHEL: An' I've been such a cat to thee, Harry.

HARRY (putting his arms round her waist): I've not seen her for two days.

RACHEL: Never mind, never mind. She's been wandering, never mind.

HARRY: Now 'er's gone.

RACHEL: Never mind, we s'll die ourselves someday, we shall. I know tha loved her, better than me, tha allers would, I know. But let me be wi' thee. (She sits down on his knee.) Let me stop wi' thee, tha wants somebody. An' I care for nowt but thee, tha knows I do.

HARRY: Should we go an' look at her?

RACHEL (kissing him): We will. (She kisses him again.) Tha's been like a bird on a frozen pond, tha has. Tha's been frozen out

HARRY: Rachel?

RACHEL: What?

HARRY: Dunna kiss me yet

RACHEL: No, I won't, I won't.

HARRY: Afterwards

RACHEL: Yes, I know, I know. (Silence a moment.) Come then, we'll go an' look at her.

She lights a candle, takes his hand. They go into the front room.

Enter SUSY.

SUSY: Where are they? I'd think they've carted off an' left th' house empty. (Calls.) Rachel! Oh my goodness! Harry!

Enter RACHEL and HARRY, both with red eyes, from the sickroom.

Oh, here you are.

RACHEL: Yes. Did you think I'd gone?

HARRY pulls on his coat and goes out.

SUSY: Yes, you said you was in a hurry.

RACHEL: I shall have to be goin'.

SUSY: I wish my father would come. Is he grumpy yet?

RACHEL: Harry? No, he's not grumpy, no.

SUSY: What? Have you made it up?

RACHEL: There was nothing to make.

SUSY: I'm glad to hear it. What about Job Arthur?

RACHEL: I never did care a bit about him or anybody else

SUSY: No, but

RACHEL: Well, but what?

SUSY: Has he asked you? Has he promised you? Our Harry?

RACHEL: Yes, not in words, but I know.

SUSY: You don't. Nurse wants him, an' Nurse'll get him.

RACHEL: She won't.

SUSY: You see.

RACHEL: Don't you fret your fat. He's not that easy to grab.

SUSY: But he's got a fancy for Nurse. He's as proud as they make 'em, an' it would just suit him to crow over us, marryin' a lady.

RACHEL: A lady!

SUSY: Well, you know what I mean. An' I believe there's summat in the will for her. My mother harped on her an' our Harry

RACHEL: An' does she know?

SUSY: She's not far off o' guessin', I'll be bound. She is a deep one, Nurse is.

RACHEL: She is. Oh, she'd soon know everything if she got a sniff. An' has your father got the will?

SUSY: No, it's in the front room.

RACHEL: Well, you should get it, an' see what it says. You should come in for something, and then

SUSY: Durst you come with me?

RACHEL: Yes, I durst come.

SUSY: Should us then?

RACHEL: Yes, let us. You could burn it if there was owt you didn't like.

SUSY: Durst you get it? (She lights a candle.)

RACHEL: Yes, if you'll show me.

They go into the next room.

SUSY'S VOICE: Doesn't it smell cold a'ready. Oh!

RACHEL'S VOICE: It does.

SUSY'S VOICE: Look, you want to get on this table. This blessed candle does jump.

RACHEL'S VOICE: I could ha' sworn tha sheet moved.

A shriek from SUSY, shrieks from RACHEL, a bump, more shrieks. SUSY rushes across the kitchen out of doors. In a moment HARRY appears in the outer doorway. RACHEL flies blindly into him.

HARRY: Whatever's up?

RACHEL: Oh Harry! Oh Harry!

HARRY: Well, what's up? What's ter got in thy hand?

RACHEL: Oh, whatever was it? Let's go.

HARRY: What wor that? What!

He starts as Patty walks mildly from the front room.

It wor nowt but our Patty.

RACHEL: I thought I should have died.

HARRY: What wor ther doin'?

RACHEL: I fell off that table. Oh, and I have bruised my arm.

HARRY: What wor you doin'? What's this?

SUSY (entering): Oh Rachel!

RACHEL: It was only Patty.

SUSY: Did you get it? Oh, look at our Harry opening it!

HARRY: Why, it's th' will. I sh'd ha' thought you'd have more about you (He reads.)

SUSY: What's it say?

HARRY: Look for thysen, if tha'rt in such a mighty hurry.

SUSY (reading): Five hundred and fifty pounds for him and Nurse Broadbanks if they marry, an' if not, to be divided between me an' him. What did I say! Would you credit, now? But there's one thing, Nurse won't have him.

RACHEL: He doesn't want her.

HARRY: She's worth a million such as you, cats as wants nowt but to lap at a full saucer. You couldna let her lie quiet for five minutes, but must be after her bit of money.

RACHEL: Indeed, I didn't want the money.

SUSY: He wants it himself, an' that's what he's been contrivin' for all along, him an' that slivin' Nurse. There's a pair of 'em.

HARRY: There's a pair of you, more like it, a couple of slitherin' cats, nowt else. No more you think of her, than if she wor a dead fish wi' the money in her mouth. But you shan't have it, you shan't, if I can scotch you.

RACHEL: Oh, Mr Sharp-shins, you think you know everything, do you? You're mistaken. It's not fair, it isn't. I only

HARRY: Tha needs to tell me nowt.

NURSE (entering): Oh, you are here! The Baroness asked me to call and see where you were, Rachel.

RACHEL: And now you've seen, you can go back an' tell her you've been.

HARRY: They've been after th' will, couldna let her rest still in her own room, but what must they do, go ferretin' for her money

SUSY: Shut thy mouth, tha's said enough.

HARRY: That I hanna. They'd claw the stuff out of her hand, if it wor there

SUSY: Hadn't we a right to see the will?

HARRY: There's a lot of right about you. Here, come here. Give us hold of it.

SUSY: I shan't.

HARRY: What! Now, Nurse, thee read it. We'n all read. Now thee read it. (NURSE reads.) Hast got it all? Tha sees?

NURSE: Yes, I understand it.

HARRY: An' what dost say?

NURSE: I say nothing.

SUSY: This is what she's been working for.

HARRY: Then let them as has worked be paid. What? I say "snip", Nurse, will tha say "snap"? Come on, "snap" me, Nurse. Say "snap". Snip?

NURSE: This is hardly the occasion.

RACHEL: He doesn't love you, Nurse. This is only his temper.

NURSE: I think, out of respect to the dead, we ought not to go on like this.

SUSY: You'll be precise and proper, all lardy-da. Oh yes, but you've got what you've been aiming at, haven't you? You've worked it round very clever. You see what carneyin' 'll do for you, Rachel. If you'd ha' buttered your words, you might ha' been alright.

RACHEL: I couldn't creep.

HARRY: No; you could slither, though.

NURSE: I'm afraid I must be going.

SUSY: Yes, you can smile to yourself, and hug yourself under your cloak in the dark. It's worth marryin' him for, five hundred and fifty pounds.

NURSE goes out.

HARRY: She's a lady, she is, an' she makes you two look small.

RACHEL: Well, Harry, you can think what you like about me: and you always have thought me as bad as you could imagine. But I only did it to help Susy, and all I've done I've done with you sleering at me. An' I shan't marry Job Arthur; I s'll go in service in Derby. An' you needn't sleer at me no more because it's your fault, even more than mine.

HARRY: A' right, ma'e it my fault.

RACHEL: As much as mine, I said.

HARRY: Dunna let me stop thee from ha'ein' Job Arthur.

RACHEL: Job Arthur's a man as can play his own tune on any mortal woman, brazen as brass, or cuddlin' as a fiddle

HARRY: Or as ronk as an old mouth organ.

RACHEL: Or like a bagpipe as wants squeezin', or a mandolin as wants tickling. He gets a tune out of the whole job lot, the whole band

HARRY: Shut up.

RACHEL: But I'll buy you a cuckoo-clock to keep you company.

HARRY: I'll buy my own.

RACHEL (flapping her arms suddenly at him): Cuckoo! Cuckoo! Cuckoo!

CURTAIN

ACT V

SCENE I

The Sunday following the last scene. The porch of Grunstom Church. The HEMSTOCKS have attended the post-funeral service. Mourners are leaving the church.

1ST MOURNER: Well, I niver knowed the likes

2ND MOURNER: What?

1ST MOURNER: Nurse Broadbanks to be axed wi' old Hezekiah Wilcox, an' Job Arthur Bowers wi' Rachel Wilcox.

3RD MOURNER: An' what about it?

1ST MOURNER: Well, I never thought Nurse would have him an' everybody said Job Arthur would never marry now.

2ND MOURNER: I'm not surprised at neither of 'em.

1ST MOURNER: I was never more taken in in my life.

Exit 1ST and 2ND MOURNERS.

SUSY: No.

3RD MOURNER: I don't call it decent, two sets of banns put up at a funeral Sunday. They might ha' waited till next week.

SUSY: I'm going to see about this.

3RD MOURNER: Yes, th' old Baron wants telling, the old nuisance, for he's nothing else.

Exit SUSY and 3RD MOURNER.

4TH MOURNER (sighing): That did me good. I'm sure I've fair cried my eyes up.

5TH MOURNER: You can't make out half the old Baron says, but he makes you feel funny.

4TH MOURNER: As if you'd got ghosts in your bowels. An' when he said, what was it?

5TH MOURNER: Was it Hezekiah Wilcox wi' Nurse Broadbanks?

4TH MOURNER: Yes, fancy 'em both bein' there to hear it. What a come-down for her.

5TH MOURNER: I dunno. The old chap's tidy well off

4TH MOURNER: But he's mushy, he slavers like a slobbering spaniel

5TH MOURNER: Well, women like that sort.

Exit 4TH and 5TH MOURNERS.

MR HEMSTOCK: I allers thought 'er'd a worn widow's weeds for me

HARRY: Dost wish it wor that road about?

MR HEMSTOCK: Nay, I non know

HARRY: Are ter stoppin'?

MR HEMSTOCK: I want ter speak ter Nurse.

HARRY: I'm goin' then.

MR HEMSTOCK: Dunna thee, tha wait a bit.

HARRY: Nay.

Exit HARRY.

BAKER (in very genteel black): Good morning, Mr Hemstock.

MR HEMSTOCK: Good morning.

BAKER: We got more than we bargained for.

MR HEMSTOCK: Yes, a bit surprisin'.

BAKER: I'm going to strike, Nurse for a mother-in-law is too much for a good thing. Why, bless me, you want to be careful what relatives you have, some you can't help, but a mother-in-law, you can.

MR HEMSTOCK: I want to speak to Nurse.

MR WILCOX (frock-coated): You've 'ad a big loss, Mr Hemstock, I've been through it myself, so I know what it is.

BAKER: Here, I say, Hezekiah, I don't mind you for a father-in-law

MR WILCOX: Hello, Job Arthur! Well, I never! I am surprised, I can tell you.

BAKER: So'm I.

MR WILCOX: But it's a glad surprise, I'd rather say "My son" to you, Job Arthur

BAKER: Hold on a bit, Hezekiah; you've always stood me as a good uncle, let's leave it at that.

MR WILCOX: I'll make you a wedding present of it, Job Arthur, that little thing, you know.

BAKER: I do, worse luck! I've pledged my soul and my honour to you, uncle, my uncle on the pop-shop side, but my body's my ewe lamb, I don't sell. Good morning, Dr Foules.

DR FOULES: Good morning. Er, excuse me, but Nurse Broadbanks has not gone yet?

BAKER: Not yet, Doctor. Here's her husband-that-is-to-be waiting for her.

DR FOULES: Ha!

MR WILCOX: Nurse has not gone yet, Doctor.

DR FOULES: Thank you.

BAKER: Let's have a look! (He peeps into the church.) Oh, oh Baron, may I speak to you?

Enter BARON, in surplice, with BARONESS and NURSE.

BARON: And you, what have you to say?

BAKER: Not much. Only there's a bit of an alteration wants makin'. Rachel's given me the sack.

BARON: I do not understand, sir.

BARONESS: He wishes to escape from his promise. He wishes to dodge Rachel.

BARON: You, sir, have you not given your word?

BAKER: And you're welcome keep it, for what it's worth. But you can't cork a woman's promise, Baroness. In short, Baron, and Mr Wilcox, Rachel has asked to be released from her engagement, hem! with me, and I have felt it my duty to release her. (He bows.)

BARON: It is an indignity to the Church. It is insult to the Holy Church.

BARONESS: I do not believe this man. It is his ruse to escape from a bond.

MR WILCOX: Yes, my lady, that's what it is, my poor girl, Nurse! Nurse?

NURSE: Let Rachel come herself.

BARONESS: She shall.

BARON (to MR HEMSTOCK): Go and bring Rachel here.

MR HEMSTOCK (shrugging): Where am I to go?

NURSE: Please, Mr Hemstock.

He goes.

BARON: Sir, I believe you are a scoundrel.

BAKER: I wouldn't deny it, Baron.

MR WILCOX: No, we know him too well, he'd better not begin denyin'.

NURSE: This is the man, Baron, the, the, the Wilcox.

BARON: What! What!

BARONESS: What do you mean, you old wicked man, insulting Nurse in this fashion?

BARON: You, you, you, sir! If you speak I will cut you down. The double shame, the double blasphemy! Ah! Leave from my sight, go, don't stir, sir, till you answer.

DR FOULES: May I ask, Nurse, if I am to congratulate you on your banns?

NURSE: I should think you have no need to ask. I am ready to die. I am so mortified and ashamed.

BAKER: Hello, I am only the mote in the eye of the Church, am I? Oh uncle, uncle!

DR FOULES: Then it is a mistake?

NURSE: Worse. It is a mean, base contrivance to trap me. I knew nothing of these banns, I could have dropped. He knows I wouldn't marry him, no, not if, not if

BAKER: You died in a ditch with your shoes on. I'm undone this time, curse it. Uncle, have a pound of flesh, will you, instead? I could spare a pound and a half, cut judiciously.

BARON: What do you say, sir?

BAKER: I'm inviting him to have his pound of flesh, instead of his two hundred pounds of money. Though it's dear meat, I own.

NURSE: What do you mean, Mr Bowers?

BAKER: I owe him £180, and he'll foreclose on our house in a couple of months. Then goodbye my bakery, and they cart my old mother to a lunatic asylum, though she's no more mad than I am.

BARONESS: And what have you done with the money?

BAKER: Paid some of my debts, Baroness, and some of it I have, as it were, eaten. So in a pound of flesh he'd get his money glorified.

BARON: What do you say, sir?

MR WILCOX: I say nothing.

CURTAIN

SCENE II

The vicarage garden wall, under which runs the path. RACHEL looks over the wall; enter HARRY.

RACHEL: All by yourself? Where's the others?

HARRY: Stopping.

RACHEL: Did they give my father's banns out?

HARRY: His'n an' thine.

RACHEL: What! Mine! Why, I told Job Arthur as I wouldn't have him.

HARRY: 'Appen so.

RACHEL: I did. An' he's never told the Baron. Whatever shall I do?

HARRY: What?

RACHEL: You don't believe as I told him.

HARRY: I believe nowt.

RACHEL: But I did, an' he's agreed. And did they ask my father and Nurse?

HARRY: Yes.

RACHEL: Oh, but I shan't have him, I shan't. The Baron'll give it me, but I shan't have him. You needn't believe me, if you don't want to.

HARRY: When did ter tell Job Arthur?

RACHEL: Yesterday. An' he was glad. He doesn't really care for me.

HARRY: Are ter having me on?

RACHEL: May I be struck dead this minute if I am.

HARRY: An' what shall ter do?

RACHEL: I don't know, go to Derby. Perhaps I'll learn to be a nurse.

HARRY: She's marryin' thy father.

RACHEL (melting into tears): Don't, tha's hurt me enough. (Dashing away her tears.) Well, I must go in and see to the dinner. Then I'll tell the Baron, and have my head bitten off. (She turns to go.)

HARRY: Are ter sure tha told Job Arthur?

RACHEL: Go and ask him.

HARRY: There's no tellin' what tha does.

RACHEL: No, there isn't, for the simple reason that I've built my house on the sand.

HARRY: How dost mean?

RACHEL: You know right enough. Well, I'll go an' warm th' rice pudding up.

HARRY: Rachel, dost care for me?

RACHEL: You'll make me wild in a minute.

HARRY: Rachel, dunna go, it's that lonely.

RACHEL: I s'll have to go and put that pudding in.

HARRY: Come down here first, a minute.

RACHEL: Come you up here.

HARRY (climbing up): Rachel.

RACHEL: What?

HARRY: It seems that quiet-like, dunna go an' leave me. I go rummagin' down i' the loose ground, to look at th' coffin.

RACHEL: Do you?

HARRY: I do. I feel as if I should have to get at her an' mak' her speak. I canna stand this dead o'night quiet.

RACHEL: No.

HARRY: Comin' out of church into this sunshine's like goin' in a cinematograph show. Things jumps about in a flare of light, an' you expect it every minute to go out an' be pitch dark. All the shoutin' an' singin', an' yet there's a sort of quiet, Rachel.

RACHEL: Never mind, it will be so for a bit.

HARRY: I canna be by myself, though, I canna.

RACHEL: There are plenty of people.

HARRY: Nay, I non want 'em.

RACHEL: Only Nurse.

HARRY: Nor her neither, never.

RACHEL: 'Appen so.

HARRY: Tha doesna believe me?

RACHEL: "I believe nowt."

HARRY: I wish I may drop dead this minute if I ever did care for her.

RACHEL (smiling): You thought you did?

HARRY: 'Appen I did think so.

RACHEL: I know you did.

HARRY: But 'er knows nowt about me, like thee.

RACHEL: No.

HARRY: Shall ter ha'e me, Rachel?

RACHEL: You want me?

HARRY: Let us be married afore the week's out, Rachel. Dunna leave me by mysen.

RACHEL: Are you in a hurry now, at the last pinch?

HARRY: Shall ter, Rachel?

RACHEL: Yes. (He kisses her.)

MR HEMSTOCK (entering): I should ha thought you'd more about you than to be kissin' there where everybody can see you, an' to-day.

RACHEL: There's nobody but you.

MR HEMSTOCK: You don't know who there is.

RACHEL: And I don't care. We're going to be married directly.

MR HEMSTOCK: It'll look nice, that will, his mother buried yesterday.

HARRY: It ma'es no difference to her, does it?

MR HEMSTOCK: Tha'rt a fawce un, Rachel. Tha's contrived it, after a'. Tha'rt a fawce un, an' no mistake. But tha's got to come to the Baron.

RACHEL: What for?

MR HEMSTOCK: Nay, dunna ask me. Tha'd better look sharp. Ma'e thy heels crack.

RACHEL. What's up now, I wonder?

They go out.

CURTAIN

&

SCENE III

The church porch.

BARON: Do not speak, sir. You have vilified me, you have held up the Church to ridicule.

MR WILCOX: I can speak, can't I?

BARON: Do not speak, you shall not, do not speak. We will not hear your voice. You are a blasphemer.

MR WILCOX: I can't see but what a Methodist's as good as a Church, whatever. What have I done, what have I done?

BARONESS: What have you done!

MR WILCOX: Whatever anybody says, there's nobody can say I've never done anything as wan't right.

BARON: What, sir, what

BAKER: Here's Rachel.

SUSY: I'll bet it's her doin's. She's the deepest I ever met, bar none.

BARON: Rachel?

RACHEL: Yes, Baron.

BARON: Who wrote to see the letter of the banns for your father and Nurse?

MR WILCOX: I did.

BARON: Scoundrel! Impostor!

NURSE: You had not the slightest justification for it.

DR FOULES: Surely, Nurse, you are flattered. A woman loves a peremptory wooing.

MR WILCOX: You accepted me on Friday night, Nurse, you know you did.

NURSE: I did no such thing.

BAKER: Now, Rachel, speak up. I say you've refused me

RACHEL: So I have.

BAKER: Of course. And I forgot to take the banns back.

RACHEL: That's your lookout.

BARON: Rachel! Ah, insolent!

BAKER: Now, my case settled, did Nurse accept your father? Of course not.

RACHEL: She did.

MR WILCOX: There you are.

NURSE: I did not. I would not demean myself. I did not.

BARONESS: This is very funny, Nurse.

BARON: I have spoken the banns.

MR WILCOX: Come now, Nurse.

NURSE: You horrid, hateful old man. You know you worked yourself into a state, I thought you were delirious, and I had to promise anything.

MR WILCOX: A promise is a promise.

SUSY: Of all the deep-uns, Rachel, you cap all.

RACHEL: What's it to do with me?

NURSE: You pestered and pestered and pestered me.

DR FOULES: All's fair in love and war, Nurse.

BARON: What were the exact words?

RACHEL: "Yes, yes. I'll marry you, if you'll settle down now and go to sleep."

NURSE: Why! What! You are an underhand thing.

RACHEL: What if I did happen to hear?

NURSE: You were listening!

RACHEL: I could hear it all.

NURSE: How hateful, how hateful!

BARON: I do not understand, explain.

NURSE: He was shamming

MR WILCOX: She's had me on a string

RACHEL: She's sniffed at him for months, wondering whether or not to lick him up.

DR FOULES: The debatable tit-bit.

BARON: I will understand this matter. Speak, Nurse.

NURSE: He shammed fever, delirium, and to comfort him, to soothe him, I said I would marry him. I thought he was raving. And I would not marry him, I'd rather beg in the streets.

MR WILCOX: Oh, but Nurse, Nurse, look here.

BARON: Silence, sir, silence. You are a base, malingering pulamiting wretch.

RACHEL: Well, she came to see him often enough, and stopped long enough

BARONESS: You cannot, Baron, blame the man for everything.

DR FOULES: A man who was delirious in fever on Friday night would hardly be disporting himself at church on Sunday morning

MR WILCOX: I'm not disporting myself.

BARONESS: I don't know. It's not much, and there are still miracles.

DR FOULES: Surely miracles are not wasted on, Methodists, Baroness?

BARONESS: I do not know, I do not know. Rachel, did you put the pudding to warm?

RACHEL: Yes'm.

BARONESS: Then it's burnt to a cinder.

BARON: You, sir, you Wilcox, are a base scoundrel.

MR WILCOX: She shall pay for this.

NURSE: I must have it contradicted, I must.

BAKER: I will contradict it, Nurse.

DR FOULES: And I.

MR HEMSTOCK: And me.

HARRY: An' me.

BARONESS: But I'm not so sure

BARON: Enough, enough. I am again a disgrace and a laughing stock. You, sir, you Wilcox

MR WILCOX: What, Baron von Ruge?

BARON: You, you, you are a scoundrel.

BAKER: It's old news.

BARON: I withdraw and refute these double banns next Sunday.

MR WILCOX: Not with my consent.

BARON: Do not speak. And in the public paper must be refutation.

NURSE: Oh, isn't it dreadful!

SUSY: Folks shouldn't shilly-shally.

BARON: And then, I have done.

DR FOULES: Perhaps you can say there was a mistake. Substitute my name for that of Mr Wilcox.

BAKER: All's fair in love and war. Substitute Mrs Smalley's name for Rachel's.

RACHEL: A change for the better is always welcome. Substitute Harry Hemstock for Job Arthur Bowers.

BARON: This is madness and insult.

DR FOULES: It is deadly earnest, Baron. Nurse, will you be asked in church with me next Sunday?

BAKER: Susy, will you be asked in church with me next Sunday?

HARRY: Rachel, shall you be axed in church with me next Sunday?

BARON: Enough, enough! Go away, I will suffer no more of this!

BARONESS: Such wicked frivolity! Rachel, go home at once to see to that pudding.

DR FOULES: We are most deeply serious, Nurse, are we not?

BAKER: Susy, are we not?

HARRY: Rachel, are we not?

RACHEL: Chorus of ladies, "Yes"!

NURSE AND SUSY: Chorus of ladies, "Yes"!

DR FOULES: Millicent Broadbanks, Arthur William Foules.

BAKER: Job Arthur Bowers, Susan Smalley, née Hemstock, widow.

HARRY: Rachel Wilcox, Harry Hemstock.

BARON: Away! Away!

DR FOULES: Baron, you should play Duke to our "As You Like It".

BARON: I do not like it, I will not.

SUSY: Then lump it.

MR WILCOX: I call it scandalous, going on like this.

RACHEL: Like it or lump it, Father, like it or lump it.

DR FOULES: You accept me, Nurse?

NURSE: I do, Doctor. (He kisses her hand.)

BAKER: You accept me, Susan?

SUSY: This once, Job Arthur. (He kisses her cheek.)

RACHEL (after a moment): Come on here, Harry. (They kiss on the mouth.)

BARON: Go away from here. You shall not pollute my church.

BARONESS: It is disgraceful.

MR WILCOX: They want horsewhipping, every one of them.

MR HEMSTOCK: Well, I must say

DR FOULES: It's "As You Like It".

BAKER: It's "As You Lump It", Hezekiah.

CURTAIN

D. H. Lawrence - A Short Biography

David Herbert Lawrence (1885-1930) is today considered to be one of the greatest novelists of the twentieth century writing in the English tongue. He is mostly remembered for his explicit examination of sensual love and sexuality. The latter orientation has subjected his oeuvre to harsh criticism from the conservative literary figures of his time and even to censorship from official authorities. Debates on the literary value of Lawrence's work have outlived him when in the case of the rather "too sensual" *Lady Chatterley's Lover* for instance, an English court had to permit of the publication of the book. However, despite censorship and the moralistic assessments of his works, D. H. Lawrence's merits have been eventually recognized by literary circles. Even critics who frown upon what they consider as the pornographic aspect of some of his writings still rank him among the most serious canonical writers and acknowledge the qualitative contribution that he has brought to the modern novel. It is also noteworthy that besides being a major novelist of the twentieth century, D. H. Lawrence was equally a talented poet, short story writer, literary critic and painter.

D. H. Lawrence was born in 1885 to a poor family living in a coal-mining town near Nottinghamshire, England. He was the youngest of four children with an alcoholic and rather irresponsible father and a mother who venerated knowledge and learning. Being a teacher herself, she wanted Lawrence to get a decent education and did her best to encourage him despite the dire financial conditions in which the family had always found itself. Although he was rather physically weak and sick, Lawrence took after his mother her passion for learning. In 1898, he was the first pupil in town to win a scholarship to Nottingham High School after spending 7 years at the Beauvale Board primary school, now known as D. H. Lawrence Primary School. He soon left high school to serve first as an apprentice clerk at a surgical appliance factory, then as a pupil-teacher. By that time, Lawrence's physical health was deteriorating as he suffered from pneumonia. Only two years after graduating from Nottingham University as a certified teacher in 1908, he lost his mother to whom he was closely related. Some accounts claim that Lawrence practiced euthanasia on his mother to end her suffering from cancer.

During these early years, Lawrence had some attempts at writing poetry and some short stories and to receive early recognition as a young talent, mainly by the *Nottingham Journal*. He also began writing his first novel to be published in 1911 under the title *The White Peacock*. Starting from 1908, Lawrence taught at the Davidson Road School in London while he continued writing poetry and fiction and dreaming of becoming a full-time writer. In London, he was introduced to established writers and publishers who started to appreciate his work and helped him publish his earliest writings. Among these people was the editor of the celebrated periodical *The English Review*. Lawrence was equally encouraged and supervised by the critic and editor Edward Garnett.

After the publication of *The White Peacock* followed by the publication of *The Trespasser* in 1912, Lawrence was working on one of his major works, *Sons and Lovers*. The latter is judged as an autobiographical novel and draws on the author's relationship with his mother. It also pictures the everyday life of working-class England. Lawrence finally resigned from his teaching position by the end of 1911 to devote all his time and energy to his writing career. After being greatly impacted by the loss of his mother and the abandoning of his teaching job, a third crucial event that would shape Lawrence's life and career happened in 1912. It was when he met and fell in love with Frieda Weekley, a German woman who was married and six years older than him. Lawrence and Mrs. Weekley fled England to live in the French-German frontier town of Metz. The couple was able to marry two years later when Frieda got her divorce. The couple spent a period of time in Germany and then moved to Italy to return to Britain on different occasions after their marriage. Later, they wandered different parts of the world, visiting different regions of Italy, Sardinia, Malta, Sri Lanka, Australia and New Wales, to ultimately sail to the United States in 1922.

This long trip around the world was probably triggered at first by the fact that Lawrence suffered from political persecution on more than one occasion in an age dominated by the general hostilities of the First World War. Indeed, in Metz, he was accused of spying for the British and was arrested to be released only after the intercession of Frieda's father. Even at home, Lawrence was suspected mainly for his non-conformist political positions, anti-militarism and unorthodox literary productions, but also for being married to a German lady at a time Nazi Germany was demonized everywhere in Britain.

Sons and Lovers was published in 1913 to realize considerable success. It was followed by the publication of *The Rainbow* in 1915. An important collection of love poems dedicated to Lawrence's love for Frieda was published in 1917 under the title *Look! We Have Come Through*. Critics see in Lawrence's poems a revival of the Romantic tradition tuned in to the modern spirit. In 1916, Lawrence started working on one of his major successes entitled *Women in Love*. Published in 1920, the novel was meant to be a sequel to *The Rainbow*, featuring recurrent characters. It paints the British society of the period while drawing on some details from Lawrence's own life. Some critics believe that the theme of homosexuality in the novel is related to Lawrence's romantic relationship with a farmer from Cornwall.

Lawrence's novels were accused of obscenity and found difficulty to be published and distributed. Nevertheless, his merit was recognized by fellow writers such as Ezra Pound and E. M. Forster.

The year 1920 also witnessed the publication of *The Lost Girl* followed by *Aaron's Rod* in 1922 and in which Lawrence provided descriptions of the different places that he had visited as an expatriate. His trip to Australia was, however, best illustrated in his 1923 novel entitled *Kangaroo* which also spoke about the troubles he had with British authorities. Most of the novels of this period bore the influence of the philosopher Friedrich Nietzsche and his theory of the "Superman." Generally, Lawrence was considered to be an elitist who did not believe in the democracy of the masses. His ideals made him the enemy of not only political authorities, but also of many a fellow literary man.

Once in America, the Lawrences were determined to remain there were it not for the author's deteriorating health condition which forced him later to return to the old continent. They acquired a property in New Mexico which is now known as the D. H. Lawrence Ranch. In America, Lawrence befriended Aldous Huxley, another important English writer who would in turn settle in Los Angeles and soon a number of other publications followed. These included *The Boy in the Bush* (1924) and *The Plumed Serpent* (1926). Lawrence became also interested in literary criticism and published a seminal work on American literature entitled *Studies in Classic American Literature*. The volume was believed to revive interest in classic American writers and American literary movements. For later critics, it was a pioneering work written by a British canonical writer on the new literary symbolism of New England, American Puritanism and American Transcendentalism. Another important critical work published by Lawrence was *Study of Thomas hardy and Other Essays*.

By 1925, Lawrence's health no longer allowed him to travel. He had to stay definitively in Florence, Italy, where he published his last books, namely *The Escaped Cock*, *The Virgin and the Gipsy* and the ever-controversial *Lady Chatterley's Lover*. After the agitation caused by the release of the latter novel and accusations of obscenity and cheap pornography, Lawrence vehemently engaged in an extraordinary campaign to defend his writings and to attack those who purport to be the defenders of morals and good taste. This is expressed in many of Lawrence's later prose works and poems. Interestingly, the act of writing with Lawrence was like an act of resistance that continued during his last days and despite his sickness and sufferings. In 1930, D. H. Lawrence was still suffering from pneumonia and tuberculosis. He passed away on March 2nd at the Villa Robermond in Vence, France.

The critical evaluation of Lawrence's oeuvre after his death wavered between praise and hostility before he was definitively established as a canonical English novelist and writer. Critics insisted only on the sexual explicitness of his works and their obsession of obnoxious language and images. However, this tendency left the floor for a more positive artistic assessment, mainly after the historical Lady Chatterley Trial after which Lawrence was proved "not guilty." The trial was a triumph for the idea of sexuality as an object of serious literary exploration and investigation. Indeed, Lawrence's work deals with sex within a social paradigm where politics, economics and aesthetics intervene. Lawrence also deals with the effects of industrialization on human behavior and the shaping of human relationships with emphasis on the role of the body as opposed to the Western overemphasis on the intellect.

Among Lawrence's attempts at non-fiction, there was a book on Freudian psychoanalysis entitled *Psychoanalysis and the Unconscious* (1922) as well as a text book for students published pseudonymously and entitled *Movements in European History*. Once Lawrence's fiction was established as a considerable contribution to canonical English literature, his other merits started to be posthumously acknowledged. These mainly included his talent for poetry as well as his respectable experience as a passionate painter. As for poetry, Lawrence left a huge bulk of material that some estimate to be around 800 poems. In fact, he had been writing poetry since his early childhood until his last years in Florence and France. Among his most famous poems, one can mention "Snake" and "How Beasty the Bourgeoisie is" while celebrated collections include *Dreams Old*, *Dreams Nascent*, *Pansies*, *More Pansies* and *Last Poems*. Like his fiction, Lawrence's verse deal with themes related to industrialization and the eternal struggle between body and mind while still focusing on and exploring sensuality.

D. H. Lawrence had also developed a constant passion for oil painting and was believed to excel in the matter mainly towards his last years. His expressionistic paintings deal with the same themes and motifs as his fiction and poetry. In 1929, a remarkable incident happened when the police confiscated thirteen of his exhibited paintings in a gallery in London. Indeed, the oeuvre was subjected to controversy among artistic circles as well as among politicians and viewpoints ranged between appreciation and praise and accusations of indecency and cheapness. The collection was later regained by its owner on the condition of not exhibiting it in England any more. After Lawrence's death, the collection found its way to Taos in New Mexico to adorn the walls of La Fonda de Taos hotel.

D. H. Lawrence had lived a controversial life and produced highly controversial literary and artistic works to be contested by generations of readers and critics. His confrontational style and his examination of taboo subjects aimed at unveiling the ugly face of false modernity and the ferocity of industrialism that victimized the human in the beginning of the twentieth century. Today, Lawrence represents one of the pillars of twentieth-century literature. The house in Eastwood where he was born and raised in poverty is now the D. H. Lawrence Birthplace and bears testimony to the merits and achievements of a man raised from oblivion to immortality and international recognition.

D.H. Lawrence – A Concise Bibliography

Lawrence's works cover a number of major forms and we have therefore grouped them under convenient headings

Novels

The White Peacock (1911)

The Trespasser (1912)

Sons and Lovers (1913)

The Rainbow (1915)

Women in Love (1920)

The Lost Girl (1920)

Aaron's Rod (1922)

Kangaroo (1923)

The Boy in the Bush (1924)

The Plumed Serpent (1926)

Lady Chatterley's Lover (1928)

The Escaped Cock (1929), later re-published as The Man Who Died

The Virgin and the Gypsy (1930)

Short Story Collections

The Prussian Officer and Other Stories (1914)

England, My England and Other Stories (1922)

The Horse Dealer's Daughter (1922)

The Fox, The Captain's Doll, The Ladybird (1923)

St Mawr and other stories (1925)

The Woman who Rode Away and other stories (1928)

The Rocking-Horse Winner (1926)

The Virgin and the Gipsy and Other Stories (1930)

Love Among the Haystacks and other stories (1930)

Collected Stories (1994) – Everyman's Library

Plays

The Daughter-in-Law (1912)

The Widowing of Mrs Holroyd (1914)

Touch and Go (1920)

David (1926)

The Fight for Barbara (1933)

A Collier's Friday Night (1934)

The Married Man (1940)

The Merry-Go-Round (1941)

Poetry Collections

Love Poems and others (1913)

Amores (1916)

Look! We have come through! (1917)

New Poems (1918)

Bay: a book of poems (1919)

Tortoises (1921)

Birds, Beasts and Flowers (1923)

The Collected Poems of D H Lawrence (1928)

Pansies (1929)

Nettles (1930)

Last Poems (1932)

Fire and other poems (1940)

Non-Fiction Books and Pamphlets

Study of Thomas Hardy and other essays (1914),

Movements in European History (1921)

Psychoanalysis and the Unconscious and Fantasia of the Unconscious (1921/1922)

Studies in Classic American Literature (1923)

Reflections on the Death of a Porcupine and other essays (1925)

A Propos of Lady Chatterley's Lover (1929)

Apocalypse and the writings on Revelation (1931)

Travel Books

Twilight in Italy and Other Essays (1916)

Sea and Sardinia (1921)

Mornings in Mexico and Other Essays (1927)

Sketches of Etruscan Places and other Italian essays (1932)

Works translated by D.H. Lawrence

Lev Isaakovich Shestov All Things are Possible (1920)

Ivan Alekseyevich Bunin The Gentleman from San Francisco (1922)

Giovanni Verga Mastro-Don Gesualdo (1923)

Giovanni Verga Little Novels of Sicily (1925)

Giovanni Verga Cavalleria Rusticana and other stories (1928)

Antonio Francesco Grazzini The Story of Doctor Manente (1929)

www.ingramcontent.com/pod-product-compliance
Lightning Source LLC
Chambersburg PA
CBHW060136050426
42448CB00010B/2152